Francis A. Schaeffer

Portraits
OF THE MAN AND HIS WORK

Francis A. Schaeffer

Portraits
OF THE MAN AND HIS WORK

Edited by
LANE T. DENNIS

CROSSWAY BOOKS ● WESTCHESTER, ILLINOIS
A DIVISION OF GOOD NEWS PUBLISHERS

Francis A. Schaeffer: Portraits of the Man and His Work.

Copyright © 1986 by Crossway Books, a division of Good News Publishers.
Published by Crossway Books, Westchester, Illinois 60153.

Photographs copyright © 1986 Sylvester Jacobs.

First printing, 1986

Cover design: Sally Cioni

Printed in the United States of America

Library of Congress Catalog Card Number 85-73846

ISBN 0-89107-386-8

Contents

PART TWO: THE PRACTICE OF TRUTH

Introduction

In Francis Schaeffer's last book, completed just a few months before his death in 1984, he asked: "What really matters? What is it that matters so much in my life and in your life that it sets the priorities for everything we do?" After quoting our Lord's words concerning the two greatest commandments from Matthew 22:37-40, Dr. Schaeffer went on to explain:

> Here is what really matters—to love the Lord our God, to love His Son, and to know Him personally as our Savior. And if we love Him, to do the things that please Him; to simultaneously show forth his character of love and holiness in our lives; to be faithful to His truth; to walk day by day with the living Christ; to live a life of prayer. . . .
>
> But it does not stop here. . . . We must acknowledge and then act upon the fact that if Christ is our Savior, He is also our Lord in *all* of life. He is our Lord not just in religious things and not just in cultural things such as the arts and music, but in our intellectual lives, and in business, and in our relation to society, and in our attitude toward the moral breakdown of our culture.[1]

The chapters which follow in this book together form a remarkable portrait of how Francis Schaeffer carried out this principle in his own life. In reading these chapters we cannot help being struck by the breadth of Dr. Schaeffer's interest—from art to law, from literature to politics, from theology to social activism. But we also see something of the profound impact he had on both individual lives and our generation, often at considerable personal cost to himself.

Each chapter reveals something of Schaeffer's[2] life and work in a unique light. Some are by leaders in various academic disciplines. Others are by people whose lives were affected in a deep and personal way by both Francis and Edith Schaeffer. Some knew Dr. Schaeffer only through his books, which nonetheless helped tranform their lives. Others found the inspiration in Dr. Schaeffer's life and work to take a strong, active and sometimes costly stand—in places as diverse as the U.S. court system, academic circles, and a peasant village in India. With essays from countries as various as Holland, Switzerland, the United States, England and India we also see something of the transcultural significance of Schaeffer's work.

Although the book is divided into two sections, the two parts form a complementary whole. Schaeffer often stressed the importance of ideas—that *ideas have consequences.* Thus the first section is titled "Knowing the Truth," and looks primarily at Schaeffer's contribution in the area of ideas. But Schaeffer also stressed that it is not enough just to "know truth" as if "truth" were something abstract and separated from the way we live our lives. Thus "Knowing the Truth," if it is genuine, leads necessarily to "The Practice of Truth" as emphasized especially in the second section. Here we see the cost of practicing the truth in the area of personal life as the Schaeffers reached out to those in need. But we also see the cost of confronting the loss of truth and morality in the wider areas of law and government. Because the two sections are complimentary, those who are more interested in the personal and activist side of Schaeffer's life may prefer to begin with the second section first. But in either case it is important to also go on to the other section, to understand Schaeffer's contribution as a whole.

(For those who may not be familiar with the work of Francis Schaeffer and L'Abri, this book can serve as a helpful introduction and starting place. Many will want to go on and read both the books of Francis Schaeffer and Edith Schaeffer, including Edith Schaeffer's biographical books *L'Abri* and *The Tapestry*, all of which are listed in the bibliography at the end of this volume. A chronology of the Schaeffers' lives, providing a helpful biographical overview, is also included at the end of this book.)

It would not be helpful to "idealize" Francis Schaeffer, and indeed he would have been very unhappy if this were the case. Consequently, as we would expect, not every author agrees with Schaeffer on every point. But neither would it be helfpul to minimize the contribution he made and thereby fail to learn from the life and work of this most remarkable man.

But if we were to learn just one thing, the most important would be Schaeffer's emphasis that if there is not spiritual reality at the center of our lives—if we do not know Jesus Christ in a personal way, living in the reality and the power of his presence—then nothing else really matters.[3] The important thing is not whether we have extraordinary abilities. God can use a dead stick of wood if He wants, as He did in the hand of Moses. As Schaeffer explained,

> Though we are limited and weak in talent, physical energy, and psychological strength, we are not less than a stick of wood. But as the rod of Moses had to become the rod of God, so that which is *me* must become the *me* of God. Then I can become useful in God's hands. The Scripture emphasizes that much can come from little if the little is truly consecrated to God. There are no little people and no big people in the true spiritual sense, but only consecrated and unconsecrated people. The problem for each of us is applying this truth to ourselves. . . .[4]

What does this mean for each of us? "We must remember," Schaeffer wrote, that in God's sight . . . only one thing is important: to be consecrated persons in God's place for us, at each moment. Those who think of themselves as little people in little places, if committed to Christ and living under His Lordship in the whole of life, may, by God's grace, change the flow of our generation.[5]

Are we willing to live under the Lordship of Christ in all areas of life, *in our own area of life*, even if this need be at great cost—whether in business, or in academics, or in the church, or in our personal life—and by God's grace, change the flow of our generation away from moral breakdown, brutal inhumanity and rebellion against God in every area of life?

Lane T. Dennis
Easter Week, 1986

Part One

KNOWING THE TRUTH

"There is no other important Christian thinker of our era who has tackled as many fundamental intellectual, philosophical, and theological issues as Schaeffer did ... and no one else has so revealed their relevance to us."

Harold O.J. Brown

Harold O.J. Brown has served as Chairman of the Division of Biblical and Systematic Theology at Trinity Evangelical Divinity School (Illinois). Currently he is Pastor of the Evangelical-Reformed Church, Klosters, Switzerland and Adjunct Professor in the Institute for Study of Human Rights, Strasbourg (France). He received the Ph.D. in history from Harvard Graduate School, and has also done graduate study at the University of Marburg (Germany) and University of Vienna (Austria). He is the author of numerous articles and six books including *Heresies* (Doubleday) and *The Reconstruction of the Republic* (Mott Media). He lives with his wife and their two children in Klosters, Switzerland.

Dr. Schaeffer and Udo Middelmann

Chapter One

Standing Against the World

by
Harold O.J. Brown
Contemporary Theology

It is hard to write about the theological influence of someone whom one knew well without including personal reminiscences. In the case of Francis Schaeffer and his work, this is entirely fitting. The influence of Dr. and Mrs. Schaeffer, and of the others who together with them made up the L'Abri family, was very personal. This can be seen in two ways: First, L'Abri's initial theological impact was not made institutionally, through the usual means—church, education, publishing, and ecumenical structures—but indirectly, through individuals whom the Schaeffers came to know and whose lives they changed. One of the fundamental principles of personal evangelism is that changed people change society. Francis Schaeffer helped a small but significantly-placed number of individuals to "be transformed by the renewing of [their] minds" (Romans 12:2), thereby proving that the changed thinking of individuals can change the Church as well as society.

Second, Francis Schaeffer's influence was personal not only in the sense that he dealt with persons and took them seriously, but also in the sense that he dealt with the great issues of our age as and because individual persons needed to take *them* seriously. There is no other important Christian thinker of our era who has tackled as many fundamental intellectual, philosophical, and theological issues as Schaeffer did. But he did this not in an effort to construct a comprehensive philosophy of history like Oswald Spengler (*The Decline of the West*) or Arnold Toynbee (*A Study of History*). Even when dealing with the big issues that were his specialty, Schaeffer treated them not as theoretical problems to be fitted into a comprehensive world view, but as questions that individual persons needed to answer in order to find meaning in their lives.

There are not many Christian thinkers who have dealt with as many of the great issues of theology and philosophy as Schaeffer did, and no one else has so revealed their relevance to us. Schaeffer treated them as vital to the understanding of our own life and its meaning, rather than as abstractions reserved for the advanced seminar. Schaeffer was unusual among deep thinkers in his desire to have ordinary people understand the great issues of philosophy and theology and their implications for ordinary living.

Schaeffer *Contra Mundum*

During the theological controversies of the fourth century, Patriarch Athanasius of Alexandria led the opposition to the Arian heresy (namely, the concept that Jesus, the Son, was "of similar nature," but not "of the same nature" as God the Father). Christianity received legal recognition from the imperial Roman government in 313. Whereas previously the cost of discipleship had been immense, after the conversion of the Emperor Constantine it became fashionable to be a Christian. This led to superficial conversions of people who were still rooted in pagan polytheism. Arianism represented a kind of accommodation to paganism, for although it used Christian terminology, it saw the Son, Jesus Christ, as a kind of subordinate divine being, something that pagan polytheists could fit into their own thought-frame. The great question confronting the church between 325 and 381 was whether it would hold firmly to its doctrine of the deity of Christ, or reach an accommodation with the Arian idea.

Athanasius was not the greatest theologian of his day. But he was the one who had the foresight and the determination to make no accommodation whatsoever to Arianism, even though it seemed that the government and the hierarchy, indeed the whole world, was against him: hence the proverb, "Athanasius *contra mundum.*" Others were prepared to make concessions which they considered reasonable; he was not. With the passage of time, more and more thinkers rallied to his position, and orthodoxy survived.

Like Athanasius, Francis Schaeffer will not be remembered as the greatest theologian of our day. Others, such as Herman Dooyeweerd, F.F. Bruce, and Carl F.H. Henry, have produced a greater mass of solid scholarship. Yet without Schaeffer's stand *"contra mundum,"* the best work of such specialized scholars might have been insufficient to check the temptations to compromise and accommodation that confronted evangelicalism after 1945 just as they confronted orthodoxy after 313.

Francis Schaeffer was converted and received his theological training between World War I and II, at a time when evangelical theology had been relegated to the fringe of academic and intellectual life. During and after World War II, evangelicalism enjoyed a renaissance—sparked intellectually by scholars such as Bruce and Henry, and spiritually by the new shape of mass evangelism under Billy Graham. Francis Schaeffer could have been part of that renaissance and quickly have attained celebrity and fortune. However, he detected flaws and compromises—not as serious as those that Athanasius saw in Arianism, and yet potentially serious enough to turn a seeming evangelical renaissance into a brief and transitory fad. Until the publication of his first two works in 1968, *Escape from Reason* and *The God Who Is There*, Schaeffer was little known in evangelical circles. From his self-chosen isolation in the Alpine village of Huémoz in the French-speaking Swiss canton of Vaud, Schaeffer at first reached only those who came to him. This comparative isolation—as well as the clarity of his own thinking—made it possible for him to see what was happening in evangelicalism, which was in danger of becoming intoxicated with its own early successes.

It was in the beginning of the 1960s that I first met Francis Schaeffer. I had heard about him two years earlier from my sister Judy (now Mrs. Roger Hull), who attended the University of Lausanne (the capital of the canton of Vaud) with one of the Schaeffer daughters, Priscilla (now Mrs. John Sandri). Among the first things that I heard from him were two predictions which seemed outlandish to me at the time: first, that Roman Catholicism was on the verge of doctrinal chaos and disciplinary collapse; and second, that America would be overrun by a wave of pseudo-mysticism from the East.

In 1961 Roman Catholicism seemed stronger and better entrenched than ever. In Boston, for example, the Paulist Fathers, an order founded to convert Protestants, were literally carrying their proselytizing campaign to the doorstep of Park Street Church, the citadel of evangelicalism in New England and a moving force behind one of Billy Graham's very first successful city-wide crusades. Who could suspect that within a few years the Second Vatican Council would let the fox into Catholicism's doctrinal henhouse, and that the Paulists would become spokemen for universalism and liberation theology? Schaeffer saw it coming.

In 1961, America's universities were devoted to science, technology, and philosohical skepticism. Who could have anticipated that within seven years the Vietnam War would sap America's science-oriented self-confidence and bring Oriental mysticism and the flower children to the university campus? Schaeffer did not foresee the war, but he saw the fragility of rationalistic Western thought and predicted its imminent self-destruction. As I recognized the clarity of Schaeffer's analysis and saw his predictions being fulfilled so much more rapidly than I believed possible, I myself ventured a prediction. In one of the first articles I wrote for a national audience, I said that Schaeffer would be for the twentieth century what Kierkegaard was for the nineteenth—all but ignored at first, but ultimately changing the shape of theology, although in a totally different way than Kierkegaard did. Even this prediction was too timid, for Kierkegaard's real influence came only decades after his death, whereas by the early 1970s, Schaeffer's ideas were beginning to pervade and to change evangelicalism. Despite this, he remained suspect among the leaders, if not the troops, of his own evangelical community. As late as 1979, for example,

Trinity Evangelical Divinity School, where I was teaching theology, rejected a proposal to devote an elective course to Schaeffer and his influence. He was not considered sufficiently important for serious consideration at an evangelical seminary!

Schaeffer's Impact

We can analyze Schaeffer's impact on contemporary Christianity under three headings: personal, theological, and social. Personally, he inspired a small group of people who in turn began to change the direction of the theological world. Theologically, he brought ideas that others might have preferred to deemphasize back into the center of theological discussion, notably, the inerrancy of Scripture and the historicity of Genesis 1—11. Socially, he challenged millions of evangelicals to take an active role in shaping their society and its values, and gave them something that the agitators could not give—a theological warrant for doing so.

Schaeffer as Personal "Mentor"   In earning a Ph.D., it is important to have a good "Doktorvator"—one who can not only teach, but help one to choose the right direction for his research and to avoid blind alleys. Schaeffer did not train doctoral candidates, but he performed the vital function of an academic "mentor" as well as a spiritual father to a small group of men and women, who may ultimately spread the influence of his thinking farther than his writings and the film series that he made. Notably, he helped many to resist the opposing temptations of neoorthodoxy and success.

The Temptation of Neoorthodoxy   During the years prior to World War II, evangelical scholarship had been forced to the fringe of academia, battered by an apparently triumphant liberalism. As evangelicals began a serious effort to make their mark in the scholarly world and to win recognition there, they suddenly saw liberal assumptions being battered and beaten down by a new movement, the neoorthodoxy sparked by Karl Barth. Rejoicing in the discovery of positive, orthodox elements in Barth's theology, many evangelicals were slow to notice that his influence was already on the wane in Europe in the 1950s. A number of evangelicals sought to claim his authority in support of their own views, hoping in this way to firm up the scholarly prestige of their evangelical convictions. As a matter of fact, Barth's fortunes were already going into Eclipse on the European continent—in part because they were in fact too close to Biblical orthodoxy, but also because of a weakness that many evangelicals missed, but which Schaeffer saw: Barth denounced liberalism, which had undermined the foundations of orthodoxy, without himself rebuilding the foundations.

Of course Schaeffer was not the only conservative Protestant who recognized this: Cornelius Van Til at Westminster Theological Seminary castigated Barthianism as "another religion," as J. Gresham Machen had done with liberalism a generation earlier. America's fundamentalists did likewise. But unfortunately, Van Til's audience was limited by the scholastic nature of his approach, and many fundamentalists discredited themselves by criticizing anyone and everyone who was trying to do serious theological thinking. For many of us who made the trip to L'Abri in the late 1950s and the early 1960s (it had not yet become a pilgrimage!), it was shocking to hear Schaeffer oppose Barth with no less vigor than he condemned Bultmann, who seemed so much more dangerous to orthodoxy. Schaeffer's warnings remain highly relevant today, twenty-odd years later, as Barth's theology is once again being cultivated by many evangelicals as an answer to the unbelief that reigns in most academic theological circles.

There is no doubt that Barth was antiliberal, and that he affirmed the central doctrines of the Christian faith. However, his failure to assert Biblical infallibility and the historicity of the Gospel accounts meant that his affirmations rested on his own charismatic authority rather than on that of Scripture. Because of his failure to shore up the foundations of Biblical authority which had been sapped by a generation of destructive criticism, Barth was not able to establish a second generation of Protestant theologians in the faith that he himself honored; his greatest influence remains among evangelicals and other conservatives who already know why they believe. There is no doubt that

Barth's affirmations *are* encouraging, but his foundations are inadequate, and it would be dangerous to take him as a theological guide. It is remarkable that Schaeffer recognized this three decades ago while some evangelical leaders today are "discovering" Barth as the answer to modern disbelief.

The Temptation of Success   Schaeffer drew a line between historic Christianity and neoorthodoxy. This in itself was shocking to many who had hoped to find valuable support there. Even more shocking was his failure to rejoice in what seemed to many the greatest triumphs of the modern evangelical movement as represented by Billy Graham and his mass evangelistic crusades, through which not a few of us had come to Christ. How could a Bible-believing Christian with a zeal for winning people to Christ criticize what was so evidently a good thing? If Barth's theology could not produce real converts (despite his personal faith) because he did not build on a sound foundation, Graham's approach, Schaeffer warned, produced a flock of pseudo-converts, because Graham (although he certainly *has* a sound foundation) did not start building there, or even at ground level, but in what Schaeffer called the "upper story"—that is, by calling for an emotional (or at best volitional) decision without giving an adequate warrant in history and reason.

Although Schaeffer's criticism of Graham's approach was not offered to a wide public, it soon became known. Several of Schaeffer's natural friends and allies, such as *Christianity Today* editors Carl F.H. Henry and Harold Lindsell, owed much to Graham. Consequently, they were put off by Schaeffer's pickiness and apparent intolerance and tended to write him off as they did militant separatists such as Bob Jones and Carl McIntire. As a result of this, they were slow to appreciate the influence that Schaeffer had among younger evangelicals, who admired him for his consistency and for his refusal to be impressed by success alone. Mass evangelism, for all its merits, is to some extent dependent on the media and on appearances. Schaeffer kept calling for solid foundations *as well as* good feelings. The fact that many of Graham's converts later went through the school of

Schaeffer's disciplined thinking has certainly given additional
strength and substance to the evangelical movement today.

Schaeffer as a Theological Pathfinder   In 1964 Schaeffer
was invited to visit New England under the auspices of the
Christian Contemporary Thought Lectures, a student-sponsored
group in Boston. The group was able to raise the sum of five
hundred dollars for his trans-Atlantic fare—not a magnificent
fee even in those days, and an indication of the small scale on
which L'Abri then operated. After dramatically successful lectures at Harvard and M.I.T., where he challenged the prevailing
skepticism and religious indifference, Schaeffer went on to
Wheaton College, which was the outstanding Christian college
in America, but also the focal point of the evangelical renaissance. (This would be documented a decade later by the establishment of the Billy Graham Center and the relocation of *Christianity Today* from Washington, D.C., to Wheaton.) At Harvard
and M.I.T., Schaeffer had proved immensely popular with the
students, but largely ignored by the faculty. At Wheaton, however, faculty members were forced to take Schaeffer seriously,
because he addressed himself to the convictions they professed
and their students demanded their reactions. The coolness of
their response was noticeable. Many faculty found it distressing
if not threatening to hear Schaeffer tell their students that certain
things that they were prepared to negotiate, or at least to deemphasize, such as Biblical inerrancy, were essentials of true
Christianity.

   Although Schaeffer did not directly attack them, other evangelical theologians, such as *Christianity Today* founding editor
Carl F.H. Henry, were troubled by his pounding attacks on the
theologians with whom they sought *rapprochement*, such as
Karl Barth, and by his uncompromising emphasis on Biblical
inerrancy. At the same time, Schaeffer's determined stand may
have prepared the way for the magazine's second editor, Harold
Lindsell—who was not otherwise a Schaeffer enthusiast—to
make the battle for Biblical inerrancy the test of evangelical
authenticity in his provocative *Battle for the Bible* (1976). Lindsell's categorical stand in favor of inerrancy created fresh ten-

sions within the evangelical establishment, but it relieved some of the pressure on Schaeffer. The Council on Biblical Inerrancy, which developed a clear and thoughtful program in defense of the doctrine of inerrancy, owes much to the virtually solitary stand of Francis Schaeffer during the 1950s and 1960s.

Schaeffer as Social Activist   During the 1960s, Schaeffer's ministry was largely based on personal contacts and centered on L'Abri in western Switzerland. After the publication of his first two books in 1968, a flood of material from his pen—the fruit of years of carefully tape-recorded lectures—as well as lecture tours in North America shifted the focus of his ministry from Europe to North America. However, he first became a really well-known figure on the American scene when he began to apply his Christian convictions in the legal and political area, something that the evangelical leadership was not prepared to do. The 1973 decision of the United States Supreme Court mandating abortion on demand, *Roe* v. *Wade*, was a kind of spark in the powderkeg for Schaeffer. For twenty years, Schaeffer had been warning that the humanistic value structure that respected individual lives would crumble to expediency as the Christian base of Western society was demolished. *Roe* v. *Wade* was unmistakable evidence that this was happening. This atrocious decision and the millions of prenatal deaths it mandated struck Francis Schaeffer as a challenge that he could not ignore.

Although the Schaeffers had been asked to lend their names to any number of causes, it was not until the founding of the evangelical antiabortion group, the Christian Action Council, in 1975, that the Schaeffer name appeared on a council of reference for any organization other than L'Abri itself. Together with C. Everett Koop, M.D., now United States Surgeon General, Schaeffer produced the film series *Whatever Happened to the Human Race?* in 1979. This film series mobilized timid and lethargic evangelicals in support for the antiabortion movement. It provided tremendous encouragement to the vast company of nonevangelical antiabortionists, including millions of Roman Catholics, making them aware of the Biblical foundation for their convictions, and stimulating them to take evangelical ideas seriously in other areas as well. However, Schaeffer's highly provocative stand against abortion further widened the gap between Schaeffer and the evangelical leadership, many of whom adopted a vacillating or even compromising stand. At the same time, it also built up a vast reservoir of support and loyalty for Schaeffer among people who were not interested in theology or the evangelical movement. Unfortunately, Schaeffer's social involvement has had the unintended side effect of giving evangelicals who find Schaeffer's views awkward a new excuse for disregarding him—now he has become "too political." (The political activism of the left-wing evangelicals is often applauded by nonleftist evangelicals because it gives evidence that evangelicals have fully arrived, while the conservative broadsides of Schaeffer—not to mention Jerry Falwell—embarrass them.)

Among his last books, it was Schaeffer's *A Christian Manifesto* that stamped him for the first time with the brand of political conservatism. (To an extent, this represents a misreading of *A Christian Manifesto*, but it is the usual interpretation of the book. The vehemence with which he excoriates current liberal dogmas and practices made him odious to liberals—indeed, more odious to evangelicals seeking acceptance among politically liberal circles than to the liberals themselves, most of whom have not paid enough attention to *A Christian Manifesto* to be alarmed by it.) This brought Schaeffer under fire from the growing party of politically liberal evangelicals—not only the radicals associated with Jim Wallis and the *Sojourners* magazine and community, but also with the more balanced liberal faction represented by Ronald Sider and Evangelicals for Social Action.

A number of evangelical scholars have attacked the historical thesis of *A Christian Manifesto*—namely, Schaeffer's conviction that the United States and American democracy were founded on Biblical values and that the erosion of this Biblical base will inevitably lead to the loss both of political liberty and of religious freedom. It is interesting to note that this attack on Schaeffer's thesis has been used to provide a measure of justification for those who were unwilling to take the risky stands that Schaeffer was demanding. In addition to writing *A Christian*

Manifesto, Schaeffer began to make common cause with politically conservative and highly visible Christians such as Jerry Falwell, who is widely if improperly regarded as a menace to freedom by left-wing evangelicals as well as by militant secularists and anti-Christians such as Norman Lear and the leaders of the American Civil Liberties Union. Schaeffer's increasingly outspoken commitment to specific conservative causes in the last two years of his life troubled some evangelicals who disagreed with him, because they recognized his influence among the general Christian public. In addition, it embarrassed others, who generally agreed with him, because they wished to avoid controversy and not to endanger their own acceptance among the general public. Consequently Schaeffer found himself once again, at the end of his life, in the position he had occupied in the 1960s, before his name became a household word—a voice crying in the wilderness.

Fully aware that his remaining time on earth was short, Schaeffer sought one last time to wrest the helm of the evangelical ship out of the hands of those whom he considered too complacent and too prone to compromise. His last book, *The Great Evangelical Disaster*, not only named individuals and institutions, but also alienated a large number of others who were not named. In this respect it resembled Harold Lindsell's bombshell, *The Battle for the Bible*, but it went beyond Lindsell's work in addressing social and legal issues as well as theological ones. For many the publication of Schaeffer's last book was simply cause for further alienation from all that he represented.

An Athanasius for Our Day

What will Schaeffer's place in church history be? In the opening paragraphs, we likened him to Athanasius of Alexandria, standing alone, *"contra mundum."* And we noted that in his final years, despite widespread admiration on the part of the general Christian public, Schaeffer again stood increasingly alone—not only against the secular world and the liberal religious establishment, but against many of the accepted leaders of evangelicalism. He was subjected to ostracism by evangelicals who were unwilling to take the clear stands which he insisted upon with increasing urgency as his death drew nearer.

Athanasius was the symbol of Nicene orthodoxy, but he alone did not create it. That required the work of subsequent generations of scholars who would not have been able to work without the security of the solid foundation, so fiercely defended by the patriarch of Alexandria. Like Athanasius, Schaeffer was a fierce "defender of the foundations," even to the point of being ostracized by the accepted leaders of evangelicalism. Yet without Schaeffer's stand *"contra mundum,"* as we noted in the beginning, the best work of these same leaders may not have been sufficient to check the temptations to compromise and accommodation that face evangelicalism today.

Like Athanasius, Schaeffer took stands—especially in his last years—which some would call intemperate and inflexible. We do not really know how Athanasius dealt with people on a personal level; it is possible that he was as severe with individuals as he was with their theology. But in Schaeffer's case, we know that the rigor of his convictions was always tempered with love and understanding in person-to-person relationships as well as in public debate. He invariably treated those with whom he deeply disagreed with consideration and love. Francis Schaeffer not only held the line for Biblical orthodoxy in his generation as Athanasius had done. What is perhaps even more important, Schaeffer showed the next generation not merely *that* they will need to take stands, but *where* to take them and *how* to do so, in Paul's words, "speaking the truth in love" (Ephesians 4:15). He has shown us that standing *"contra mundum"* is an essential part of being *"pro Christo."*

"Francis Schaeffer . . . has done more than anyone else in recent memory to restore the humanities to their true function. . . . [He showed] that the deepest values and greatness of the arts and culture have their origin in their Lord, who in saving human beings, also saves the humanities."

Gene Edward Veith, Jr.

Gene Edward Veith, Jr., is assistant professor of English at Concordia College, Wisconsin, and holds a Ph.D. in English from the University of Kansas. He is the author of two books, *The Gift of Art* (InterVarsity Press) and *Reformation Spirituality: The Religion of George Herbert* (Bucknell University Press), with a third book forthcoming. He has also written for *Christianity and Literature* and *Christianity Today*. He lives with his wife and their three children in Cedarberg, Wisconsin.

After a Wedding

Chapter Two

The Fragmentation and Integration of Truth

by
Gene Edward Veith
The Humanities

When Francis Schaeffer sought to understand the spiritual problems of twentieth-century human beings, he turned as a matter of course to the humanities, to considerations of art, history, and culture. For Schaeffer, one of the major problems of modern thought, and one of the biggest obstacles to Biblical orthodoxy, is the tendency to fragment truth—to split off ordinary life from religious doctrines, to separate nature from grace. Schaeffer, in his method as well as in his philosophy, worked to pull truth together.

"In our modern forms of specialized education," he writes, "there is a tendency to lose the whole in the parts, and in this sense we can say that our generation produces few truly educated people. True education means thinking by associating across the various disciplines, and not just being highly qualified in one field, as a technician might be."[1] Elsewhere, he amplifies the point:

> Today we have a weakness in our educational process in failing to understand the natural associations between the disciplines. We tend to study all our disciplines in unrelated parallel lines. This tends to be true in both Christian and secular education. This is one

of the reasons why evangelical Christians have been taken by surprise at the tremendous shift that has come in our generation. We have studied our exegesis as exegesis, our theology as theology, our philosophy as philosophy; we study something about art as art; we study music as music, without understanding that these are things of man, and the things of man are never unrelated parallel lines.[2]

Such a concern for the way knowledge fits together—for the interrelationship between art, history, culture, and what they reveal about "the whole man—has traditionally been the goal of the humanities. Ironically, the humanities have become as specialized as any other academic field, and their practitioners have become "technicians." Francis Schaeffer was not a cultural "technician," but he has done more than anyone else in recent memory to restore the humanities to their true function. In doing so, Schaeffer has encouraged orthodox Christians to engage the modern world in its own terms. Christians need not fear secular thought; instead, secular thought desperately needs what Christianity has to offer.

Shaeffer's works had an impact on countless students of the humanities. In this essay, I will offer myself as an example. I will then suggest some specific contributions Schaeffer has made to the humanities and answer some objections that have been made to Schaeffer's approach. My thesis is that Schaeffer is both a popularizer and a sophisticated Christian thinker, a cultural critic and an apologist for culture, an advocate for the humanities who, by untangling them from a conceptually limiting humanism, gives them a stronger grounding in the infinite, personal God.

Placing the Humanities on Solid Ground

I remember as a graduate student in English first stumbling upon some books by Francis Schaeffer in a Christian bookstore near campus. At the time I was a Christian, but not particularly an evangelical one. I had been caught up in the exhilarating world of graduate studies. Not only was I experiencing the intellectual excitement of new ideas, but I was also becoming involved with people who had the same sorts of rather eccentric interests that I did. I treasured my Christian faith, but it had little to do with my academic interests, my new vocation of teaching, or, for that matter, with the everyday concerns of my life. In Schaeffer's terms, religion was an "upper-story" realm that had little to do with the "lower-story" realm in which I lived, worked, and thought.

Schaeffer, though, was a different bird entirely. Here was someone engaged with the arts, philosophy, and history, as I was, who insisted on relating them to Christianity. He was not simply integrating them into a nice homogeneous whole—as in, "See how all great works of literature are really Christian at heart." I had heard that before, but did not really respect it much. To homogenize Christ and culture seemed to distort both. Schaeffer, though, was taking both Christ and culture seriously, setting them against each other, finding points of agreement and divergence, letting them battle it out.

From my own studies, it appeared that Schaeffer really did understand the Enlightenment, Romanticism, and Existentialism. He might omit a few details, but he understood and sympathized with what was often skimmed over in my classes, but which the great thinkers and artists themselves usually admitted: their despair. To this he opposed the "Christian world view." I did not realize at the time that there was such a thing—that there could be a Christian view of reality just as there is a romantic, a materialistic, and an existential view of reality. Schaeffer's explanations of the infinite-personal God, of the nature of His creation, and His revelation to us through human language, through an absolute, inerrant Bible, blew away my rather anemic, homemade liberal theology.

As I was reading Schaeffer, I started trying him out in my graduate studies. He was not only helping me understand and appreciate Christianity; he was also helping me understand and appreciate my academic discipline. In this moment of intellectual history, the field of humanities, which once itself had the task of integrating human knowledge, has been having trouble integrating itself. History is not sure whether it is an art or a social science; art is torn between aesthetic formalism, divorced from meaning, and social engagement; literary criticism is not even sure there are any self-contained texts to analyze. Underneath all of the surface controversies were the deeper worries that people in my field only talked around: What is the value of the humanities? If human beings are absurd and doomed animals trapped in a meaningless world, why study them? If there is no meaning in life, what business do we have speaking of meaning in literature? It does seem that poetry, art, and history are important, but how can we explain that importance in an age in which values are relative? In what sense, comprehensible to the twentieth-century mind, can we say that Milton is "greater" than Harold Robbins, or that students should take a humanities course instead of a class that will help them make lots of money?

Schaeffer, in showing how works of art can reveal the deepest of human problems and how history and philosophy can help diagnose the origins of these problems, makes the humanities important indeed. In rejecting modern relativism and in insisting on the objectivity of values, Schaeffer is in effect defending the classical liberal arts as a body of knowledge against the modern pragmatism and materialism that threaten to destroy them. Moreover, by emphasizing that God created the objective universe according to His will, declaring it to be "very good," Schaeffer justifies all objective knowledge. In emphasizing that human beings are created in the very image of God, which gives them intrinsic value in themselves, Schaeffer places the humanities on solid ground.

In the meantime, I started reading the Bible and accepting its authority. I found that evangelical Christians on campus, a group I had never had anything to do with before, could be more interesting to talk with than many of my secularist friends who were caught in the dead ends of bohemianism and the posturings of secular humanism. Schaeffer's emphasis on the Reformation led me to read Luther and other Reformers, who opened up for me more deeply the fullness of grace that is offered in the gospel of Jesus Christ. I became a card-carrying evangelical.

Schaeffer's ideas were helping me not only as a Christian, but also as a scholar. My studies of literary history were becoming more and more coherent since I had something to measure it with. Schaeffer's perspective worked interestingly in class discussions and in conversations with my fellow graduate students. I began to see the strength of the Biblical world view for the humanities. I began to experiment with "world view criticism" in my own scholarship. I started teaching a course on Literature and Religion in which I could pursue some of my new interests in the relationship between faith and art.

Schaeffer, I suspect, had a similar impact on hundreds of college students. Whereas college has traditionally been a place where students lose their faith, in the last several decades it has been a place where students find their faith. Schaeffer's Christian intellectualism and its appropriation by various campus ministries deserve, under the Holy Spirit, much of the credit. Whereas the tendency has often been for conservative Christians to "separate themselves" from "worldly" culture, thereby leaving the intellectual world with its enormous influence to the unbelievers, Schaeffer showed that orthodox Christianity, uncompromised and undiluted, is strong enough to challenge secularist thought in its own territory.

Humanities Without Humanism

For Schaeffer, the nature and the value of the humanities reside not in the greatness of man, but in the reality of God. According to the Bible, God is both infinite and personal. Eastern religions teach the infinity of God, but their God is impersonal, a force and a unity void of personality and therefore without love. Pagan religions often speak of personal gods, but they are only glorified human beings, projections of human vices and uncertainties, too limited and finite to be of much use. The triune God of the Scriptures, on the other hand, is both the infinite, omnipotent Creator of the universe, and the Heavenly Father who cares personally for each of His children.

When God created human beings, He made them "in His image" (Gen. 1:26). That is, He made these limited creatures to be "personal," just as He is personal. God is conscious, rational, creative, and free; He has a moral dimension; He loves. Therefore, human beings too have consciousness, a rational mind, creativity, a moral dimension, the longing for freedom and love. The Fall has spoiled what human beings were meant to be—now we are twisted, rebellious, and lost. Still, we are persons, not animals and not machines. Our personhood points upward to God. Ironically, modern thought tends to debase this personhood. Human beings are only animals. The qualities that make life valuable—love, goodness, purpose—are only illusions. Worse, human beings are only machines—a collection of knowable physical impulses, a closed, determined system. For some reason, the secular humanists who hold these views often think of themselves as exalting man. Christianity, on the contrary, has a reason for valuing people and their accomplishments.

For Schaeffer, the humanities are evidence and expressions of the personal dimension of man, which is shared with God Himself. Human beings perceive beauty, discover truth with their minds, enact history, love their families, and live by values because they were created in the Image of the infinite and personal God. Human beings can communicate to each other through the almost miraculous medium of language. Similarly, God communicates to us person to person through language (the written word of the Bible) to reveal what we could never know on our own—that God in Jesus Christ has actually entered our history in space and time to retore the personal relationship between ourselves and our Creator and to make possible the wholeness of personality that we were intended to enjoy.

Because our "personal" qualities are what we share with God, they are very precious. The humanities—painting, music, literature, philosophy, history, and the rest—express the human condition in its very essence. To understand contemporary human beings, one must study their music, their art, and their language.

Schaeffer believes in the unity of truth. The doctrine of the inerrancy of Scripture, which he insisted upon so strenuously, does more than simply insure doctrinal orthodoxy, as important as that is in an age that can substitute any irrational experience for religious truth. In the pages of the Bible, taken as normatively true on every level, Schaeffer finds a world view that brings together the "divided field of knowledge"[3] that characterizes the modern experience and that leaves us vulnerable to uncertainty, religious madness and despair.

The arts, philosophy, and culture, however, have often set themselves up as a religion in themselves. Many people look to aesthetic experience for "transcendence," "values," and "the meaning of life." The vocabulary of aesthetic criticism is filled with displaced theological terms. Schaeffer refuses to allow the humanities to be a religion. As such, he often runs roughshod over some of the conventional pieties of us humanities professors. He is not simply trying to expose evangelicals to the broadening perspective of the arts—he exposes art to the broadening perspective of evangelicalism. He does not make out the artist to be a mystical source of superior wisdom and insight—for him, artists are our representatives, not our high priests. Schaeffer holds artists to account for the content they convey and urges audiences to be discerning, not merely appreciative.

In untangling the humanities from the theology of humanism, Schaeffer makes them even more valuable. The personal dimension of human beings, the source of all the humanities, comes to nothing if we are autonomous, alone in an empty, impersonal universe. But this personal dimension in all of its creativity and imagination points upward to the personal God, who is the true source of everything that the humanities value. In addressing the "whole man" and the whole culture with the message of Christ, Schaeffer recasts the humanities and establishes them on a stronger foundation.

Schaeffer's Contributions

Besides giving a conceptual grounding for the humanities, Schaeffer has made a number of specific contributions. Christian scholars in the humanities, and even their non-Christian colleagues, can learn a great deal from Schaeffer's ideas and also from his methods. Schaeffer's influence in the classrooms of Christian colleges and in the renaissance of evangelical scholarship is already profound, and it has not yet reached its full potential. Four contributions seem especially significant: his interdisciplinary methodology; his development of world-view criticism; his focus on the Reformation; and his Christian critique of culture.

The Integration of Knowledge   Schaeffer was not only a theorist of how truth and knowledge can be unified. He was also a practitioner of this unity. To read Schaeffer, on almost any topic, is to leap from theology to art criticism to the history of philosophy to political theory to pop-culture. The first chapter of his book on pollution, for instance, starts by describing a personal visit Schaeffer had with a scientist in Bermuda. He then quotes a poem, takes on Charles Darwin, cites a song by the rock group The Doors, discusses a history professor's article in *Science*, and works with allusions to St. Francis of Assisi and Zen Buddhism, all in only five pages.[4] In his theological discussions, he will range from the philosophy of St. Thomas Aquinas to the films of Bergman and the music of John Cage, with analyses of Samuel Rutherford's political theories and recent Supreme Court decisions along the way.[5]

Many people find this interdisciplinary jumping about confusing, and many scholars wish Schaeffer would linger more on his examples and explain them more fully. The point, though, is that for Schaeffer, there really is a unity of truth, and human expressions of every type really do all point to the essence of the human condition. Therefore every piece of knowledge can be related in some way to every other piece of knowledge. Schaeffer argues that we must stop separating nature from grace, the "lower story" from the "upper story," the various academic disciplines from theology and from each other. Perhaps more impressively, he showed us, in practice, how this can be done.

Liberal arts colleges are concerned with integrating the various disciplines by means of the humanities. Christian liberal arts colleges are concerned further with "integrating" faith and learning, with somehow relating the whole range of academic courses, from English composition to calculus, from music appreciation to accounting, to Christian doctrine and practice. How should we then do this? Christians in academia can look to

Schaeffer not only for a theory, but for something much more difficult to find: a model.

World-View Criticism   Schaeffer was also a pioneer in a particular way of analyzing a work of art to show how it reveals the world view of its creator and of its age.

Schaeffer's world-view criticism is quite similar to "the new historicism," an important trend in contemporary scholarship. Whereas traditionally history has been used to illuminate a text, it is also possible to use a text to illuminate history. Details about Renaissance England—Shakespeare's life, the customs of his audience, the political context of the Elizabethan court—can certainly help us understand *Hamlet* better. The new historicists turn the emphasis around: reading *Hamlet* can open up for us the depths of Renaissance England, uncovering its psychology, its presuppositions, its contradictions, and the cultural dynamic that is accessible to us in no other form than through its art.

Schaeffer is not an academic critic, of course, and the purpose of his books does not allow him to spend time on "close readings" and formal analysis of works of art. Still, his practice of interpreting works of art as a way of unveiling the deepest values and assumptions that underlie the artist and the culture can be extremely fruitful and illuminating. At its best, this approach sheds light not only upon the world view that is being studied, but also upon the work of art. Schaeffer's drawing our attention to the gigantic hands of Michelangelo's *David* gives us a striking insight into the optimism of Renaissance humanism and, at the same time, causes us to marvel at the richness and subtlety of a magnificent work of art.[6] As we read Schaeffer, details about works of art— Giotto's figures standing on tiptoe, the irony of Bach's "Brandenberg Concertos" playing in the background of Bergman's film *The Silence*—are thrown into sudden significance.[7]

Schaeffer takes seriously the explicit or implicit content of the work of art—he often strenuously disagrees with what the artist is conveying, and yet he does so with profound sympathy. Quot-

ing a nihilistic poem by Dylan Thomas, Schaeffer underscores
our kinship with the poet and becomes almost overcome with
compassion:

> This poem is by a fellow human being of our genera-
> tion. He is not an insect on the head of a pin, but
> shares the same flesh and blood as we do, a man in
> real despair. . . . It is not good enough to take a man
> like this or any of the others and smash them as
> though we have no responsibility for them. This is
> sensitivity crying out in darkness.[8]

The tendency for many Christians is to either attack artists for
being "non-Christian," burning their books lest we be corrupted
by them, or to baptize the artists against their will, finding deep
underlying Christian messages in atheist witers such as Beckett
and Camus. Schaeffer does neither. Instead, he takes the artists
seriously, trying to understand deeply and sympathetically what
they mean and feel and believe.

Far from limiting a reader's taste or restricting the artistic
canon to a few doctrinally pure artists, world-view criticism as
practiced by Schaeffer actually opens up the whole range of the
arts to the Christian. One does not go to a work of art to agree or
disagree with it, but to understand the depths of personality that
it expresses and to encounter the world view that it signifies. It
involves what C.S. Lewis describes as "receiving" rather than
"using" the work of art.[9] According to Lewis, "the specific value
or good of literature" is that "it admits us to experiences other
than our own."[10] Thus, it is possible "to enter into other men's
beliefs (those, say, of Lucretius or Lawrence) even though we
think them untrue."[11]

Schaeffer's world-view criticism is not the only way to approach art, of course; nor does he deny purely aesthetic appreciation.[12] His major emphasis, though, which is in the best
tradition of the humanities, is to integrate the arts with the other
realms of knowledge and with life.

The Centrality of the Reformation Another contribution Schaeffer has made to the humanities is his reemphasis upon the Reformation as a pivotal moment in Western culture. Schaeffer is sometimes accused of overromanticizing the Reformation, of skimming over its problems and difficulties; but in presenting Reformation Christianity as a model for a Biblical integration of truth and of life, he has performed an important service for Christians in the humanities.

Christian scholars of the twentieth century have generally looked to the Middle Ages as the high point of a specifically Christian culture. Truly an Age of Faith, the medieval period was a time in which nearly everyone agreed on the supernatural reality of God, and this unified conception of life is reflected directly in the art, the literature, the social life, and in the very order that underlies them all. The glories of the Gothic cathedrals, the splendor of the pageantry, the soaring poetry of Dante, all testify to a different, more spiritual mindset than does our own fragmented, faithless age. The Reformation, although accomplishing many needed reforms, unfortunately managed to break the Christian unity of Western culture, tragically opening the door to individualism and secularism, to the splintering of Christendom and leading into the stark barrenness of the modern world.

Such a view, promoted by many great Christian scholars such as T.S. Eliot, has been somewhat problematic for Protestants in the humanities. It has driven many of them to the Episcopal Church, which seems more medieval in its liturgical worship and sacramental theology. Some have adopted Catholicism. Many more have stayed in their Protestant churches and lived with the tensions between their own traditions and those of Christian scholarship.

Schaeffer, in his resolute evangelical theology, criticizes the Medieval "Age of Faith" for its works-righteousness, for erecting ecclesiastical barriers between the ordinary worshiper and Christ, and for segmenting human life into sacred and secular vocations, thereby separating nature from grace. In its place, he offers the Reformation as the time of true unity and balance in

Christian history. The Reformation doctrine of the priesthood of all believers meant that everyone—a farmer, a merchant, an apprentice, a serving-girl—could approach God directly, and that such occupations were true vocations from God and valued spheres of Christian service. The Reformation exalted ordinary family life. It promoted the education of the masses so that everyone could learn to read the Word of God. The freedom of the gospel began to lead to political freedoms. Although the Reformation has its problems, its mark on the West was a profound one, and involved more than mere theological disputes, leaving its mark on all of culture. In lifting up this period of Christian thought, Schaeffer is urging a model of a culturally and Biblically alive Church for modern Christians to emulate.

Thus for Schaeffer, Rembrandt is a better model for Christian artists than the medieval icon-makers. Rembrandt integrated nature and grace, presenting in his Biblical illustrations a real, historical Christ amidst a real world of trees and inns, dusty roads and rough waters. Rather than painting Christ triumphant on a golden throne staring down at us from a background of beaten gold, Rembrandt painted Jesus as the Bible narratives portray Him, on a human scale. Perhaps more significantly, Rembrandt, refusing to separate the sacred from the secular, made ostensibly nonreligious paintings as well. Like Leo Jud, the iconoclast, he was interested in painting the images of God as made by God Himself;[13] that is, he was interested in painting human beings. Rembrandt's portraits of families and merchants, children and old women, suggest the value of them all as bearing traces of the Image of God, who is the source of all personality.

For Schaeffer, Bach is a more fruitful mode for Christian musicians than the ethereal composers of the Gregorian chants. Bach's music combines incredible harmony, imaging both the individualism and the integration that characterizes Reformation spirituality. All of his magnificent music, whether a majestic Scripture chorale for church or a light "secular" piece of dance music for the court, Bach did for the glory of God, ending his compositions with the notation "S.D.G."—the Reformation motto: "To God alone be the glory."[14]

By emphasizing the Reformation, and flexible, wide-ranging Christian artists such as Rembrandt and Bach, Schaeffer is calling modern Christians to a more comprehensive view of the Christian life, one that has an effect on every part of existence. The Reformation did not restrict Christianity to the "upper-story" level of mystical experience. Rather, the Reformation church interacted with and revolutionized politics, music, the arts, family life, and the culture as a whole. Clearly, Schaeffer would like the contemporary church to do the same, applying Biblical principles to every sphere of life to heal the modern schizophrenia and despair.

Today, scholars are rediscovering the importance of the Reformation for Western culture. My own work in literary history, which is concerned with the Reformation's impact upon English literature, was directly infuenced by Schaeffer, and there is a good deal of research to be done. The centrality of the Reformation is not simply a theme for academic scholarship, though. For Schaeffer, the Church of the Reformation, which was both conservative and revolutionary, radically Biblical and radically contemporary, deeply spiritual, yet engaged with the world, is a symbol and a model for contemporary Christianity.

A Christian Critique of Culture   The Reformation was a time for great cultural achievements, but it was also a time for smashing idols. In the same way, Schaeffer carries on the Reformation tradition of iconoclasm, tearing down revered humanistic philosophies and sacrosanct figures such as Aquinas and Dante, Kierkegaard and Barth. Schaeffer's ability to call into question aspects of the humanities is also part of his contribution.

For Schaeffer, there is such a thing as a Biblical world view, which our culture either moves towards or falls away from. For the past several centuries, and especially in the modern world, we have fallen away from Christian presuppositions. The resulting confusion and despair, the crisis in values and meaning, are at the root of our social and spiritual problems.

Some say this diagnosis is simplistic, but in its broad outlines it makes possible an incisive critique of Western culture. We are so caught up in our world and in our history that it is difficult to stand outside it, which is necessary for truly objective observation. For Christians, Schaeffer tries to untangle the Biblical elements from the "worldly" elements, and in doing so helps us understand both of them more clearly.

The contemporary scholar Herbert Schneidau has argued that this willingness to criticize culture and the capacity to refuse to accept human artifacts as absolute is at the essence of Western culture and that it comes to us from the influence of the Bible. Mythological cultures such as that of the Canaanites almost never change—social structures are sanctioned by the religious codes, so that everything is sacred. It is almost impossible for mythological cultures to criticize their leaders because there are no transcendent values by which they may be judged. The ancient Hebrews, on the other hand, held even their kings accountable to the transcendent Law of God. Because God alone is absolute, no human creation could be made ultimate; thus, all human creations could be subject to scrutiny, judgment, and change. The Bible, according to Schneidau, "demythologizes us," banishing the demons from nature, thus opening up modern science, throwing down the god-kings, thus making possible modern political freedoms and social change. Because we tend to fall into myth, we continue as a culture to need the Bible.[15]

Although he would not agree with all of Schneidau's analysis, Schaeffer, in applying the Word of God to culture and in calling into question humanist myths and heroes, is performing the role of the ancient Hebrew prophets. This role is essential not only for our religious lives, but also for our cultural lives. Schaeffer calls those in the humanities to question what they have been taught, to look closely at the moral and spiritual dimensions of the philosophies and works of art they treasure, and sometimes to stop taking them all so seriously.

Schaeffer refers to the "flow" of history and culture;[16] for some of us, that flow is like a torrent which can wash us away. In offering Christians in the humanities a perspective by which they can judge and interpret the "flow" of history and culture,

Schaeffer helps them to do what the great figures in the humanities have always done—to swim against the stream.

Objections to Schaeffer

Many Christians in the humanities object to Schaeffer's findings and to his approach. Christian scholars at Christian colleges are sometimes more critical of him than Christian scholars at secular colleges. The former are often trying to "open up the minds" of their rather narrow and close-minded Christian students. For them, Schaeffer's critiques get in the way of what they are trying to accomplish, giving their students only more excuses to disdain Western thought. Christians at secular colleges, though, are often trying in a different way to open up the minds of their secularist colleagues and students, so that Schaeffer seems a welcome ally. Apart from points of theology and specific details of interpretation, several broader objections deserve to be considered.

Schaeffer is often accused of overgeneralizing, of making sweeping conclusions on the basis of very small and not always very representative details. He marches through history without mentioning the exceptions and the facts that do not fit in with his thesis about Western thought. As a result, Schaeffer seems to many scholars rather limited and one-sided in his analyses. There is more to a poet such as Dante than his platonic obsession with Beatrice. St. Thomas Aquinas was a great philosopher and theologian, with many positive contributions to Christian thought; yet, because he is accused of separating nature and grace, something Aquinas was actually trying to overcome, Schaeffer saddles him with the blame for fragmenting modern thought. Many think Schaeffer is similarly unfair in his handling of Kierkegaard, Barth, and others.

What should we think of these objections? First of all, overgeneralizing is inevitable in any panoramic view of human history and culture. The same sort of broad strokes can be found in any work that tries to integrate something so large and complex as Western culture. Schaeffer never distorts any modern thinker the way Lord Kenneth Clark and even Will and Ariel Durant distort the Reformation, for example, and they are professional scholars who should know better. Schaeffer is looking at the "flow" of history, not its details. He is interested in the forest, not the trees.

Sometimes Schaeffer misses a few trees, but his map of the forest is basically reliable. In my own work, I have occasionally disagreed with him. For example, Schaeffer generally put forward representational, realistic art, such as that of the Reformation, as being more in tune with the Bible than nonrepresentational, abstract art. In my own research into the Bible's view of art, inspired by Schaeffer, I found that abstract art would probably have been more congenial to the ancient Hebrews than representational art. Many Hebrews, perhaps neglecting the sanction for representational art in the Temple, feared creating any likeness of anything in heaven or in earth or under the earth (Exod. 20:4). This Commandment, however narrowly interpreted, channeled art into new directions. The Hebrews decorated their pottery and tapestries with intricate nonrepresentational designs, initiating a tradition of monotheistic abstract art. The idea that art is supposed to imitate the external world comes from Greek aesthetics, which has dominated Western art.

And yet, my disagreement is superficial. Schaeffer is correct in a more basic sense: modern abstractionism *does* come out of the view that the external world is meaningless, and that the artist must create a personal nonrational meaning from within the self. Most modern artists *themselves* speak in these terms. Reformation art does reveal the balance between nature and grace that Schaeffer is advocating. Christian artists, on the basis of the Bible, can certainly work in abstract styles, or any other style as Schaeffer himself shows,[17] but modern art did develop pretty much the way Schaeffer describes it.

There may be things of value in the Middle Ages, in Kierkegaard, and in Barth which Schaeffer overlooks, but he is surely right that existentialism has fractured our sense of reality and that it has seriously distorted modern theology away from Biblical orthodoxy. The idea that ordinary life is meaningless, and that we must look for meaning in a leap into some nonrational mysticism is certainly a prevailing assumption in the twentieth century. Because meaning and the religious sphere is held to be nonrational and not related to ordinary reality, anything can be used to give meaning to life. I know many brilliant, rational intellectuals who believe in astrology, Yoga, reincarnation, and herbal medicine. The fact that the same people can be both rationalistic and superstitious, that people of the twentieth century are too sophisticated for orthodox Christianity, but can believe in horoscopes, visions of cultists, and dire warnings from UFOs—all of this is evidence of a catastrophic split between "the real world" and what people look to for meaning in their lives. This sort of religious irrationalism is a danger also in conservative churches, but it runs rampant, as Schaeffer acutely shows, in the most respectable academic liberal theology.[18] There is more to Western culture, of course, than this conceptual shift in what truth means; but it is a profound topic, whose roots Schaeffer finds as far back as Aquinas, and which shapes much of Schaeffer's analyses.

What may disturb many scholars more than his thesis is that Schaeffer is not particularly "scholarly" in the way he presents his ideas. He jumps from one assertion to the next without supporting any of them in depth. He relies more on broad secondary sources than on close analysis of primary texts. His style is loose and controversial, seldom developing an idea in detail with academic rigor by citing evidence, offering documentation, and qualifying his findings.

The academic world of today is a world of specialists. Schaeffer is a "generalist" in the classic tradition of the humanities. He did not master the details of every field that he discussed—theology, philosophy, literature, political science, art, history, scientific theory. Who could? Certainly, Schaeffer manages better than almost anyone else; the range and the breadth of his interests is remarkable, but he was never interested in being mistaken for a specialist.

Schaeffer admits that "I am not a professional, academic philosopher." He leaves it to "the most academically oriented philosopher" to "deal with more of the necessary details."[19] Schaeffer is not so much a scholar as he is a thinker. He is not studying the theology of Karl Barth; he is advancing a thesis which he thinks can be illustrated by the theology of Karl Barth. Technical scholarship is certainly important, but so are the original insights, the provocative hypotheses that demand, interpret, and shape research—and it is here that Schaeffer's contribution is so significant.

Some Christian philosophy teachers have become annoyed with Schaeffer for pedagogical reasons. Students who have read Schaeffer often come to class thinking that they now know everything there is to know about Western philosophy. I can certainly sympathize with those professors. There are few things more frustrating than students who know a little bit about one subject and are so arrogantly convinced that they need to learn nothing more that they become unteachable. And yet there is one thing worse: students who care nothing for the subject. The Christian students who read Schaeffer will be concerned for philosophical issues. They may be dogmatic, but in taking dogmas seriously they will have started to think in a philosophical way. Teachers at Christian colleges sometimes do not realize that although Christian students may have closed minds, so do non-Christian students. In fact, non-Christian students are often far worse, with their minds closed even tighter, because they have so little interest in abstract ideas. The academic world is starting to notice this. One secular professor, lamenting "this indifference to this cynicism about ideas" on the part of his students, notes one exception: "The only active intellectual endeavor I find happening right now among young people is Christianity. The so-called born-again Christians are the only kids I find defending what I consider solid abstract-type thinking."[20] Christians who have read Schaeffer do not know everything about philosophy, but that they are becoming concerned about and interested in philosophy and the humanities as a whole is surely profoundly significant and may be largely due to Francis Schaeffer and his influence in the evangelical community.

Such criticisms in fact suggest a major contribution Schaeffer has made to the humanities: he has popularized them. Academic elitism is perhaps the worst enemy of the humanities. When the humanities are made into an esoteric mystery, they are inevitably impoverished and made irrelevant. The humanities must stay in contact with "humans." Today, art is often in the hands of an elite group of critics and artists who despise the taste of "ordinary people" and are excruciatingly condescending to their audiences. Philosophy has become so technical that it has divorced itself from the normal human impulse to wonder about things. Human history belongs not simply to professional historians, but to individual human beings.

I remember leading a series of discussions on the film *How Should We Then Live?* for a little small-town church in Oklahoma. Few of the people watching these films were well-educated. Most of them were sophisticated in their faith, but not in ways the academic world would respect. Yet here they were, urgently and perceptively discussing Michelangelo and Rousseau. They were seeing in modern art reflections of problems their children were having with their friends. They were noticing the clash of world views evident in political discussions and in TV shows. They were understanding how modern ways of thinking and everyday problems have their origin in the past and how they themselves are a part of a dynamic Western culture. These people were recovering their heritage. They were being equipped for ministering as Christians to the modern world. In the best and most practical sense, they were practicing "the humanities."

Schaeffer is a popularizer, but he is also more sophisticated than many scholars give him credit for. Schaeffer offers not so much a philosophy as what many contemporary theorists would describe as a meta-philosophy. He does not offer simply another philosophy in the never-ending sequence of one philosophy giving place to another one. (As in the scene in *How Should We Then Live?* in which he stands on the beach with a stick, drawing in the sand diagrams representing the different philosophical systems, crossing each one out as the next philosophy takes its place.) Instead, he offers a philosophy about philosophy, a way to look at philosophy as a whole.

In his writings Schaeffer confronts some of the more subtle intellectual issues of the day. Many theorists are recognizing the fundamental role of language in human thought, but they are also questioning its adequacy. Schaeffer too insists that language is essential to personality, going on to emphasize that a personal God would therefore communicate to us through human words as we have them in Scripture. Communication, whether with God or with other people, can, through the medium of language, be "true" without necessarily being "exhaustive," a distinction that I think goes a long way towards solving some of the subtler problems of "post-structuralist" linquistics.[21]

Many modern scholars are looking for the inner contradictions that they say are built into language and texts, and thus try to "deconstruct" them. Schaeffer anticipates their technique in a much more profound way by looking for the inner contradictions that are built into human beings alienated from God. Because Christianity is true, it accurately describes reality as it is. Nonbelievers, insofar as they are human beings living in the real world, cannot be consistent to their own presuppositions. Schaeffer's method of evangelism is to probe for the contradictions in the unbeliever's life and so "take the roof off," leaving the sinner, pushed to the edge of despair, broken and naked to the grace of God.[22] Schaeffer is not concerned with deconstructing texts; he is deconstructing sinners.

The Integration of Truth

Schaeffer contributed to the humanities by opening them up to a theological perspective, which alone can justify and give meaning to the personal dimension of human beings. He also contributed to theology by opening it up to the humanities, showing that an understanding of art and culture can help the church effectively address the issues of the modern world. Schaeffer was interested in all of knowledge, in every dimension of the human being. He managed to achieve what many in the humanities desire in theory, but never really accomplish: the integration of truth.

The keystone of this integration is the Bible, and his purpose was to reach the modern world with the gospel of Jesus Christ. "To me," writes Schaeffer, "there is unity of all reality, and we can either say that every field of study is a part of evangelism (especially useful to certain people in the world); or we can say that there is no true evangelism that does not touch all of reality and all of life."[23] Schaeffer was an evangelist to the humanities. He "took the roof off" by exposing the contradictions of the conventional humanism that has tended to dominate the field. He went on, though, to show that the deepest values and greatness of the arts and culture have their origin in their Lord, who, in saving human beings, also saves the humanities.

"Francis Schaeffer was the instrument through whom hundreds of thousands of people became conscious of [the] intellectual dimension of the Christian faith, of the importance of philosophy, . . . of the message that ideas have consequences."

Ronald H. Nash

Ronald H. Nash is Professor of Philosophy and Religion at Western Kentucky University. He holds graduate degrees from Brown University (M.A.) and Syracuse University (Ph.D.). Dr. Nash is the author or editor of fourteen books including *Process Theology, Christianity and the Hellenistic World, Liberation Theology, Christian Faith and Historical Understanding, The Concept of God, Social Justice and the Christian Church*, and *The Word of God and the Mind of Man*. He has also published in such journals as *The Intercollegiate Review, The New Scholasticism, Augustinian Studies, The Journal of Private Enterprise, Christianity Today*, and *The Reformed Journal*. He is a Fellow of the Christianity Today Institute.

Chapter Three

The Life of the Mind and the Way of Life

by
Ronald H. Nash
Philosophy

Philosophy plays a central role in the work of Francis Schaeffer. Schaeffer recognized that important developments in philosophy had helped to push modern man into his present predicament. In order to point the way out of these problems, it would first be necessary to show the critical points at which philosophy, and the culture of the West that was influenced by it, took the wrong direction. It was Schaeffer's method then to look at the broad flow of philosophy and culture in the West, and to focus upon the key thinkers at critical points where these problems were most apparent. His approach was to take a panoramic view of intellectual history and culture in order to achieve a broad perspective on the past and to understand how specific critical points shaped the urgent cultural, moral, and philosophical issues of the day.

Schaeffer's Method and Objectives

Given Schaeffer's method and purpose, it is not surprising that a number of Christian philosophers have been critical of his treatment of philosophy. Some have complained, for example, that his discussion of such philosophers as Thomas Aquinas, G.W.F. Hegel, and Soren Kierkegaard has misrepresented or at least oversimplified their views. Furthermore, some have used this kind of criticism to write off Schaeffer's work as a whole, using their points of disagreement with him in particular areas as grounds for invalidating his overall approach.

These objections need to be dealt with on a number of levels: First, no one's work is without problems and limitations—whether Schaeffer's, my own, or anyone else's. Not surprisingly I do find problems in some of Schaeffer's interpretation of particular thinkers. But these problems, some of which we will look at in the course of this chapter, clearly are not such that they invalidate his basic approach or his apologetic strategy. A second problem is that Schaeffer's own thought is often not represented fairly. This can happen in two ways: Some of those who have been influenced by Schaeffer have appropriated his ideas in a way that is much too simplistic; thus some of the criticism directed at Schaeffer should really be redirected toward them. But it is also true that Schaeffer has not always been dealt with fairly and accurately by his scholarly critics, even though they should know better. Such distortions of Schaeffer's work—by either his followers or his critics—have only added confusion to the matter. Third, there is a natural tension between Schaeffer's method and purpose as compared to those of the academic specialist in philosophy. The specialist, of course, is interested primarily in the in-depth understanding of a specific area of knowledge. As a generalist, however, Schaeffer is interested in a general understanding across the broad field of knowledge. To the extent that these two objectives run at cross purposes there is bound to be tension. But it would be wrong, as often happens, for either the generalist or the specialist to write the other off.

It is important to recognize that Schaeffer did not consider himself to be a specialist who thought he was providing the final word on philosophy, and it would be unfair, as some have done, to criticize Schaeffer on these grounds. Schaeffer's work should be judged in its proper context which includes the audience he was addressing and the specific objectives he was attempting to reach. A large chunk of Schaeffer's audience were conservative Christians who are notorious for the reluctance or refusal to consider the intellectual dimensions of their faith. In my opinion, *anyone* who can lead hundreds of thousands of people, as

Schaeffer did, to drink even briefly at the waters of philosophy has performed an important service. And I find it more than a little ironic that some evangelical intellectuals who are now so critical of Schaeffer admit that Schaeffer's work provided the initial stimulus for their own beginning explorations of philosophy.

When Schaeffer's writings about philosophy are viewed in their proper context, one will also recognize how clearly Schaeffer admitted his limitations in this field. Schaeffer viewed himself as an evangelist, not as a philosopher. He wrote:

> I am not a professional, academic philosopher—that is not my calling, and I am glad I have the calling I have. . . . But when I say I am an evangelist, it is not that I am thinking that my philosophy, etc. is not valid—I think it is. . . . That is not to say that all my answers are correct. Nor is it to say that the more academically oriented philosopher cannot deal with more of the necessary details. But what I am saying is that all of the cultural, intellectual or philosophic material is not to be separated from leading people to Christ. I think my talking about metaphysics, morals and epistemology to certain individuals is a part of my evangelism just as much as when I get to the moment to show them that they are morally guilty and tell them that Christ died for them on the cross. I do not see or feel a dichotomy: *this* is my philosophy and *that* is my evangelism. The whole thing is evangelism to the people who are . . . [lost in the sense] that they do not have any answers to the questions of meaning, purpose, and so on.[1]

Since many modern men and women will not listen to the gospel until they see its intellectual relevance and recognize the hopelessness of their non-Christian intellectual commitments, Schaeffer saw the need for a "pre-evangelism" that would help to remove intellectual hindrances to conversion.

But it is important that Schaeffer's many students realize that his books do not contain the final word on the philosophers about whom he wrote as Schaeffer himself acknowledged. As a philosopher, I am glad that many of these people know something about Aquinas, Kant, Hegel, Kierkegaard, and Sartre and are able to place them within the history of Western thought. For those who have made this start because of Dr. Schaeffer's work, it is important that they do what Schaeffer himself would want—namely, to continue their study and make corrections when necessary.

In an effort to be both helpful and constructive, the rest of my chapter will do the following: First, I will summarize briefly how Schaeffer's treatment of certain philosophers fits in his overall system. Second, I will point out ways in which Schaeffer's analysis has sometimes been misused and misapplied, and how his case could be strengthened by introducing some qualifications and changes in focus. Third, I will offer my own interpretation of the German philosopher Friedrich Nietzsche, who—in my judgment—is the clearest example of the philosophical and cultural trends which concerned Schaeffer. Finally I will offer some concluding reflections on what I believe are the more important contributions Schaeffer has made to Christian thought at the close of the twentieth century.

An Overview of Schaeffer's Thought

In agreement with some other Reformed thinkers, Schaeffer believed that Thomas Aquinas (1225-1274) adopted certain positions that had the effect of starting Western man down a path that would lead eventually to modern secularism. The first mistake Aquinas made, according to Schaeffer, was to think that the human intellect was unaffected by the Fall. This, Schaeffer suggests, left man's autonomous intellect free to develop natural theology and to reason about nonrevelational matters (philosophy) without any help from or dependence upon God's grace or revelation. Schaeffer thought that Aquinas had effectively divided reality into two layers or stories, Nature and Grace. The difference between Nature, the lower story, and Grace, the upper story, is the distinction between creation and creator, the natural and the supernatural, earthly temporal things and heavenly eternal reality, the visible and the invisible world, man's body and man's soul. In the centuries after Aquinas, Nature (the lower story) began to overwhelm the sphere of Grace. Aquinas's apparently innocent move of separating Nature and Grace laid the groundwork for the growing secularism of the West that followed. Like a heavy semitruck without brakes rushing down a steep mountain road, this secularism has continued to gain momentum through the centuries after Aquinas. The natural sphere's gradual overwhelming of the heavenly can be seen in the history of art, science, philosophy, and religion. By the time of Isaac Newton, nature was viewed as a machine encompassing all of reality that operated independently of God.

While Aquinas had left room for divine revelation in the area of Grace, the Enlightenment eliminated the supernatural because of its failure to satisfy the test of human reason. By the time we reach Rousseau, Kant, and other figures of the Enlightenment, Aquinas's distinction between Nature and Grace had become transformed into a separation between Nature and Freedom. This split can be seen perhaps most clearly in Immanuel Kant's distinction between the phenomenal world (the world of nature as it is studied by science) and the noumenal world. Because Nature was thought to operate in a deterministic, machine-like way, there seemed to be no place left for such vitally important human characteristics as freedom. Kant thought he solved this problem by distinguishing between the deterministic world of science where there is no human freedom (the phenomenal world) and the noumenal world where freedom, immortality, and God become postulates of practical reason. The sphere of Freedom was a result of man's understandable desire to carve out room for himself against the encroachment of the impersonal machine of Nature. But the obvious tension between Nature and Freedom raised the question of how both could be reconciled by reason.

Schaeffer saw Hegel and Kierkegaard as the two dominant figures in early modern philosophy whose thought helped bring the Western world to its present state. For Schaeffer, Hegel

(1770-1830) was the symbol of modern man's rejection of absolute truth in favor of relativism. On this interpretation, Hegel rejected the absolute distinction between two opposites (A and non-A)—called "the anti-thesis"—in favor of the synthesis in which all views and theories contain moments of final truth that merge into higher truths and so on. Short of the final and ultimate synthesis, all "truth" is relative. Human knowledge must evolve and progress until, over a long period of time, it reaches the final whole which alone is *the* Truth. "Truths" encountered along the way to the final whole are only partial truths which are quickly negated and superseded by constantly higher truths. For Schaeffer, Hegel's position was a clear repudiation of "the anti-thesis," the absolute difference between truth and error, between good and evil. Since Christianity is a world view in which these absolute differences are crucial, modern men and women who are tainted by relativism will never be able to see why Christianity makes sense until they can recover respect for the antithesis.

Kierkegaard (1813-1855) became Schaeffer's symbol of modern man's elimination of reason as a unifying factor of human life. While Hegel at least believed that conflicting areas of human knowledge and claims about reality could be synthesized by reason, Kierkegaard "came to the conclusion that you could not arrive at synthesis by reason. Instead, you achieved everything of real importance by a leap of faith. So he separated absolutely the rational and the logical from faith. The reasonable and faith bear no relation to each other. . ."[2] For Kierkegaard, on this reading, meaning and truth have no intrinsic connection with reason and knowledge; they are attained by an irrational leap of faith.

The adoption of Hegelian relativism and Kierkegaardian irrationalism are the two primary sources of the despair that afflicts modern men and women. There is no longer any hope of discovering absolute truth and with the recognition of that loss comes inevitable meaninglessness and hopelessness. Nothing matters any more; since it makes no difference, do whatever you want. Such relativism and irrationalism is readily apparent in modern culture, for example, in its art, music, philosophy, and theology.

The Misuse of Schaeffer's Work

Schaeffer's overview of how Western philosophy developed and how this led to a growing sense of despair in the West is both creative and provocative. It brings together a broad sweep of history into an interpretive framework that can be helpful in understanding the past and our own times. At the same time there are many who will not agree with various aspects of Schaeffer's interpretation or with his approach as a whole. I believe, however, it is possible to retain the value of Schaeffer's general approach and basic insights. At the same time his case could be strengthened by introducing some qualifications and by refocusing some of his analysis.

I would suggest, first, that a stronger case could be made by starting the analysis of where Western civilization went wrong with the Enlightenment. By beginning with the Enlightenment the argument is much simpler and more direct. Nor do the important steps in Schaeffer's argument require going back beyond the Enlightenment to Aquinas. In my judgment it is best not to interpret Aquinas as a proponent of any radical separation between Nature and Grace,[3] as Schaeffer is often criticized of doing. Actually, Schaeffer's critique of Aquinas is much more subtle than this. For example, Schaeffer wrote in *Escape From Reason*:

> Thomas Aquinas (1225-74) *opened the way* for the discussion of what is usually called "nature and grace.". . . Aquinas's view of nature and grace did not involve a complete discontinuity between the two, for he did have a concept of unity between them. From Aquinas's day on, for many years, there was a constant struggle for a unity of nature and grace. . . . Aquinas certainly hoped for unity and would have said that there was a correlation between natural theology and the Scriptures. . . .[4]

Thus Schaeffer did not himself see Aquinas as a "proponent of a radical separation between Nature and Grace." Schaeffer's main point concerning Aquinas is that a principle of separation between Nature and Grace was introduced in Aquinas's theology, and this principle bore bitter fruit in centuries to come. But again, if one starts with the Enlightenment, there is no need to become sidetracked by a debate over how Aquinas fits into the scheme. It is interesting to note that the Enlightenment is in fact where Schaeffer started the analysis in his last book. In commenting on the breakdown of moral absolutes in our culture today Schaeffer wrote:

> How did this come about? . . . Here . . . I would refer to just one aspect of this—that is, the influence of the Enlightenment. . . . It is important to understand what the views of the Enlightenment were, for they have left a radical mark upon religion in America up to this day. . . . [As] defined in *The Oxford Dictionary of the Christian Church*, "The Enlightenment combines opposition to all supernatural religion and belief in the all-sufficiency of human reason. . . ." The central ideas of the Enlightenment stand in complete antithesis to Christian truth. More than this, they are an attack on God himself and his character.[5]

The discussion of Aquinas, however, raises a further issue concerning some who have "read a little Schaeffer" and become an instant expert in philosophy. For example, some have applied Schaeffer's critique in such a way as to suggest that Aquinas is *the singular cause* of modern unbelief; or that Hegel is *the singular cause* of moral relativism in our time; or that Kierkegaard is *the singular cause* of twentieth-century irrationalism. This, of course, is not only an inadequate approach to philosophy; it is also unfair to Schaeffer's own work and fails to take into account the nuances of his own analysis.

In response to those who have misused Schaeffer's work in ways similar to this, I would suggest a number of corrections and qualifications which would be helpful. First, instead of seeing various individuals as a kind of exclusive *cause* in the development, for example, of irrationalism or relativism, it would be better to treat them as illustrations or key figures who are representative of more general trends in the culture. In a similar vein, Hegel should not be seen as the originator of relativism or as the individual cause of its modern expression. Relativism existed in various forms at the beginnings of Western philosophy among the Sophists whom Socrates and Plato debated. Once this is recognized, however, Hegel can properly be seen as the prime exemplar of post-Enlightenment relativism. I would also caution against arguing that the movement of Western thought flows only in a straight line toward meaninglessness and despair, or toward relativism. For example, such relativistic systems as pragmatism and existentialism are fading from the scene. Many of the philosophers I read these days are advocates of what Schaeffer called the "anti-thesis," and a good percentage of these are Christians. Although there is a continuity in the flow and development of ideas, it is not always in one direction. In looking at the entire history of philosophy, it is probably better seen how man has continued to repeat the same basic mistakes again and again as he sought truth apart from God.[6]

In concluding this section I would mention briefly Schaeffer's critique of Kierkegaard. It is well known that Schaeffer was highly critical of Kierkegaard's understanding of faith and reason. From this it is often assumed that Schaeffer thought Kierkegaard's work was totally worthless. It is suprising then to read Schaeffer's relatively balanced statement at the beginning of his discussion of Kierkegaard in *The God Who Is There*:

> Kierkegaard was a complex man and his writings, especially his devotional writings, are often very helpful. For example, the Bible-believing Christians in Denmark still use these devotional writings. We can also be totally sympathetic to his outcry about the deadness of much of the Church in his day. However, in his more philosophical writings he did become the father of modern thought. This turns upon his writing of Abraham and the "sacrifice" of Isaac. Kierkegaard said this was an act of faith with nothing rational to base it upon or to which to relate it. Out of this came

the modern concept of a "leap of faith" and the total separation of the rational and faith.[7]

Thus Schaeffer did see considerable value in Kierkegaard's works, and felt that both his devotional writings and his critique of spiritual deadness in the Church would be profitably read and studied by Christians. But what about his views on Kierkegaard's understanding of faith and reason? Is this in fact a fair reading of Kierkegaard? The view which is gaining most support today among scholars in philosophy does not see Kierkegaard as having made a complete separation between faith and reason. Most recent work has recognized that although Kierkegaard did emphasize the importance of subjectivity in religious commitment and the limits of a rational evidence in bringing one to faith, he stopped short of making a complete separation between faith and reason.[8] In defense of Schaeffer, however, his position is not without support among scholars in philosophy. Although this position has been in decline during the last two decades, respected philosophers have read Kierkegaard in much the same way as Schaeffer.[9] The point here is that although Schaeffer's view of Kierkegaard is in decline, it is not without scholarly support and that he was more balanced than he is often given credit. Actually this poses an interesting challenge to Schaeffer's followers. As questions arise concerning Schaeffer's views in this area,[10] those whom he has influenced would do well to go beyond Schaeffer's own critique and address the issues in a scholarly manner and settle for themselves whether or not he was correct. I believe this would also have been Schaeffer's own wish.

Nietzsche's Analysis of Western Culture

As suggested earlier, there is something to be said for treating the Enlightenment as the starting point for man's latest push towards autonomy. In this connection, Friedrich Nietzsche (1844-1900) offers one of the better illustrations of the modern trend toward irrationalism, relativism, and moral breakdown.

It is a bit surprising that Schaeffer did not make more use of

Friedrich Nietzsche in his discussion of the West's drift toward nihilism. In many respects, Nietzsche is a better alter-ego for Schaeffer than either Hegel or Kierkegaard, but it is more difficult to get inside Nietzsche's system. Once this is done, however, Nietzsche's own diagnosis of Western civilization parallels that of Schaeffer at many points. Where they differ, naturally, is in regard to their recommendations about what should be done.[11]

A key passage in Nietzsche's writings is a story in his book *The Gay Science* that he entitled "The Madman."[12]

> Have you not heard of that madman who lit a lantern in the bright morning hours, ran to the market place, and cried incessantly, "I seek God! I seek God!" As many of those who do not believe in God were standing around just then, he provoked much laughter. Why, did he get lost? said one. Did he lose his way like a child? said another. Or is he hiding? Is he afraid of us? Has he gone on a voyage? or emigrated? Thus they yelled and laughed. The madman jumped into their midst and pierced them with his glances. "Whither is God?" he cried. "I shall tell you. *We have killed him*—you and I. All of us are his murderers. . . . God is dead. God remains dead. And we have killed him. . . ."
>
> Here the madman fell silent and looked again at his listeners; they too were silent and stared at him in astonishment. At last he threw his lantern on the ground, and it broke and went out. "I come too early," he said then; "my time has not come yet . . . this deed is still more distant from them than the most distant stars—*and yet they have done it themselves.*"

In many respects, this text is the key that can unlock the meaning of Nietzsche's philosophy. His startling statement that God is dead was not an assertion of his own personal atheism. It was not so much a piece of metaphysical speculation about the nonexistence of God as it was a diagnosis of the civilization of his day. What Nietzsche meant was that men no longer believe in God. For all practical purposes, Western man has destroyed his faith in God; he has killed God.

It is interesting to note that the very men who began by ridiculing the madman's search for God were also shocked by his apparent blasphemy. Nietzsche's point has even more force in our own society where with few exceptions, men live their lives as if there were no God and yet still carry on a profession of being religious. In Nietzsche's dramatic picture, there is something tragically absurd about the man who is shocked by someone else's atheism when it is impossible to discover any genuine religious faith in him. For the average American today, as for the average individual in Nietzsche's Germany, it simply makes no practical difference whether God exists or not.

But Nietzsche's main concern was not religion but ethics. Even though men no longer believed in God, they had not yet become fully conscious of the extent of their unbelief. Moreover, the morality of the Western world was still grounded on the presuppositions of the Christian faith. Nietzsche realized that if civilization were to survive, men needed standards and values by which to live. But he also realized that traditional morality, that is, the morality of Western Europe, went hand in hand with the Christian faith. What will happen, Nietzsche was asking, when men see the incongruity between their rejection of God's existence and their acceptance of a morality grounded on the nature and being of God? What will happen when men finally understand that the foundations of Western morality are no longer solid rock but only sinking sand? Schaeffer's one answer to such questions can be found in *Whatever Happened to the Human Race?* This is when, Schaeffer suggests, the "unthinkable" becomes the "thinkable." Nietzsche feared what would happen when modern man finally realized that he was continuing to cling to a morality, the foundations of which he had abandoned years before. Nietzsche's special term for what would happen next is *nihilism*.

Nihilism would be a condition in which all ultimate values lose their value. That is, traditional moral values will become obsolete with the knowledge that their logical ground (God) is nonexistent. Thus, Nietzsche feared, when men awaken from their sleepwalking, civilization will collapse and nihilism will result. If Nietzsche's diagnosis is correct, what is needed is a new foundation of morality; the old one has been destroyed. Much of his philosophy should be understood as an attempt to provide just such a new foundation—in Nietzsche's terms, "a revaluation of all values." As Nietzsche has his prophet Zarathustra say, "To value is to create; hear this, you creators! Valuing itself is of all valued things the most valuable treasure. . . . Change of values—that is a change of creators. Whoever must be a creator always annihilates."[13] In other words, the creation of new values must be accompanied by the annihilation of old ones. And so Nietzsche attacked traditional morality like a man possessed. Christian morality, he wrote, is the morality of weak, decadent people. What we need in its place is a morality of strength and power—*the will to power*. In place of what he called the "slave-morality" of Christianity, Nietzsche proposed to substitute a "master-morality" in which the chief virtues would be strength, dominance, and the will to power.

> What is good? Everything that heightens the feeling of power in man, the will to power itself. What is bad? Everything that is born of weakness. What is happiness? The feeling that power is growing, that resistance is overcome.[14]

The final result for the few who would understand Nietzsche and were able to follow him would be the Superman (*Ubermensch*). This term which occurs so often in Nietzsche's writings is better translated as the "Overman." What Nietzsche was trying to say is that man in his present condition is only a bridge to a higher form of life. "I teach you the Overman. Man is something that shall be overcome. What have you done to overcome him?"[15] Again he wrote: "Man is a rope, tied between beast and Overman—a rope over an abyss. A dangerous across, a dangerous on-the-way, a dangerous looking-back, a dangerous shuddering and stopping. What is great in man is that he is a bridge and not an end."[16] Behind man is the beast from which he came; ahead is the being he can become if only he allows Nietzsche to guide him. But if man should falter, look back and fail to move ahead to the Superman, he will fall from his precarious perch into the bottomless pit of nihilism. Students of Schaeffer will recognize his own warnings about meaninglessness and despair.

But it is still not clear what Nietzsche meant by "the will to power" and "the superman." The Superman, or Overman, is the strong man whose will refuses to submit to the values and standards of others, *especially God*. He is the powerful man who creates his own values. Nietzsche's strong man never says, "I ought." That is he never submits to rules laid down by God or anyone else. Rather, the Superman is the person who says, "I will!" It is a mistake to read an advocacy of moral libertinism into Nietzsche's words. Nietzsche would warn that a man who is dominated by his lusts, who cannot control his passions, is not a strong man—is hardly an examplar of the will to power. The Superman will be master both of himself and of his environment. Actually, Nietzsche taught the value of an action lies in the agent and not in what he does. Nietzsche did not really care whether a man lived a life of self-control or licentiousness as long as it was done out of strength and power, *as long as it was a reflection of his autonomy*! Nietzsche's Superman begins to remind us of the ethics of the early Jean-Paul Sartre who did not care what choices people made so long as they were their choices. In Sartre's case, however, he lived long enough to repudiate such a view.[17]

Nietzsche's parable of the madman who proclaims the death of God is an apt picture of the religious bankruptcy of the West. In spite of pious professions to the contrary, most men and women go on acting as if God does not really exist. In such a condition, for all practical purposes, God *is* dead since men and women don't really believe in Him. In an effort to save society from the nihilism that would follow the discovery of the death of God, Nietzsche was willing to destroy the old Christian foundations of morality and substitute a new naturalistic, autonomous basis of value.

It is interesting to see the extent to which Schaeffer would agree with Nietzsche's diagnosis. Schaeffer certainly taught that when any culture reaches the point that God becomes dead (because the people in that culture no longer believe in God), the only way to save that culture is to confront its men and women with their unbelief and secularism and challenge them to place their faith in the living God who is there. While Schaeffer's diagnosis of his culture was similar to Nietzsche's, his prescription was the opposite. If men no longer believe in God, it will not do to bury God. We must bring men and women to the point where, by God's grace, they can once again have faith in the living God.

While such other modern philosophers as Marx, Sartre, and Dewey urged men to abandon the supernatural assumptions of the past and ground their lives, values, and culture on naturalistic premises, Schaeffer and others recognize that naturalism is a false god and that naturalism can only produce the very nihilism that terrified Nietzsche. Thus Schaeffer urges a return to the controlling assumptions of a Christian world view grounded in a genuine personal religious faith.

Schaeffer's Contributions

The major significance of the philosophical element in Schaeffer's thought rests in his remarkable ability to recognize which philosophical lessons needed comment, criticism, or application before which particular audiences, and his equally striking capacity to communicate this often difficult material to hundreds of thousands of people. While this communication often required an enormous simplification of the material, every philosophy professor knows how important it is to vary one's presentation in accordance with the level of the audience.

As a philosopher, I am gratified to see Schaeffer insisting that the Christian faith dare not ignore philosophy. One of evangelicalism's greatest weaknesses has been its tendency to ignore or even despise the life of the mind. Inattention to philosophy is one reason for the weakness of so much evangelical training in theology. As Schaeffer wrote:

> Our theological seminaries hardly ever relate their
> theology to philosophy, and specifically to the cur-
> rent philosophy. Thus, students go out from the the-
> ological seminaries not knowing how to relate Chris-
> tianity to the surrounding worldview. It is not that
> they do not know the answers. My observation is that
> most students graduating from our theological semin-
> aries do not know the questions.[18]

Though philosophy and religion often use different language
and often arrive at different conclusions, they deal with the same
questions, which include questions about what exists (metaphysics), how humans should live (ethics), and how human
beings know (epistemology). Schaeffer helped large numbers of
Christians to see that philosophy matters. It matters because the
systems that oppose Christianity are philosophies that use philosophical methods and arguments. It matters because Christianity
has an intrinsic connection to philosophy and the world of ideas.
It matters because philosophy is related in critically important
ways to life, culture, and religion. The history of philosophy
contains crucial turning-points that have helped lead the human
race to its present crisis. Ideas have consequences.

Schaeffer also helped people understand the importance of
understanding Christianity and its competitors in terms of world
views. Christianity is not simply a religion that tells human
beings how they may be forgiven. It is a total world and life
view. Christians need to recognize that their faith has important
things to say about the whole of human life. Once Christians can
understand in a systematic way how the options to Christianity
are also world views, they will be in a better position to justify
their choice of Christianity rationally. In this connection, one of
the most valuable things anyone can learn from Schaeffer concerns testing competing world views in the laboratory of life.
Non-Christians, Schaeffer argued, cannot live lives consistent
with their non-Christian world views. Every non-Christian
must, sooner or later, cheat by borrowing elements from the
Christian world view. This insight is an important tool in pre-
evangelism as Christians invite people to consider whether their

world view really is one that they can practice consistently in their daily lives. Schaeffer also recognized the importance of helping people become conscious of the presuppositions of their world view and the world views of others. He kept searching for the philosophical roots of a person's thought. He wanted his readers to dig below the surface and recognize the basic presuppositions that control the thinking of Christians and non-Christians. He also wanted to help people to see the logical implications of various presuppositions and show them how non-Christian presuppositions are incompatible with important convictions that we all hold about morality, the world, and ourselves. Before anyone rejects Christianity, Schaeffer argued, he ought to try it out. He ought to accept the presuppositions of the Christian faith and the world view that flows from those presuppositions. He should then see if Christianity does not make more sense of his inner and outer worlds than his own non-Christian presuppositions. Christianity not only offers an interpretation of all of life that makes sense and that gives meaning to life and the world, it is a system that people can live consistently. In order for the secularist to live his life, he must continually borrow elements from the Christian world view.

Finally, I appreciate Schaeffer's insistence that Christianity has an intrinsic connection with reason. Christians should not be irrationalists. Faith is not a blind, irrational leap in the dark. The Christian faith is not at war with logic, philosophy, or science. Christianity has an inescapable relationship with truth; Christian faith has an intellectual content.[19]

Francis Schaeffer was the instrument through whom hundreds of thousands of people became conscious of this intellectual dimension of the Christian faith, of the importance of philosophy, of the significance of world views and their presuppositions, of the message that ideas have consequences. The last thing Schaeffer would have wanted is for these people to regard his writings as the final word on the subject. Now that his work has brought them to the table, it is important that they continue their study of philosophy and its inter-relationships with the Christian faith. This would be the greatest compliment that any student of Schaeffer could pay him.

"Schaeffer is among the few wide-ranging religious thinkers who has been truly radical in his approach to culture ... Schaeffer's diagnoses ... are courageous not only in that they require an unflinching look at reality; but also in that, if taken seriously, they necessarily induce a sense of anxiety which can only be overcome through faith."

James Hitchcock

James Hitchcock is Professor of History at St. Louis University (Missouri) and holds the Ph.D. in history from Princeton University. He is well known for both his scholarship and journalism. He is the author of seven books, including *What Is Secular Humanism?* (Servant) and *Catholicism and Modernity* (Crossroads). Dr. Hitchcock lives with his wife and their four children in St. Louis, Missouri.

Chapter Four

Taking the Disease Seriously

by
James Hitchcock
History and Culture

Although modern liberal religion has insistently called on believers to involve themselves in all aspects of culture, it is ironic that one of the modern Christians who has done that most assiduously has been an orthodox evangelical whose familiarity with the modern scene provides the basis for one of the most devastating critiques of religious liberalism ever mounted.

Even those who do not agree with Francis Schaeffer's conclusions can hardly help but be impressed with the range of his learning. Few modern theologians, even the giants of liberalism like Paul Tillich, have shown the familiarity with philosophy, art, politics, popular culture, and many other things which are characteristic of Schaeffer's writings.

The Liberal Delusion

Schaeffer also pays modern culture the compliment of taking it seriously in a way liberals who are enthusiastic about it often do not. Many attempts by religious liberals to "understand" modern culture are banal. There is endless verbiage about "depth," "anguish," "piercing vision," and other clichés employed to show that the critic "appreciates" what he is studying without commiting himself to specific judgments about it. Religious liberals begin with the dogmatic assumption that there is, finally, no real antipathy between modern culture and Biblical faith. And in order to "prove" this, they find it necessary to ignore some of that culture's most obvious manifestations, drowning them in a sea of well-meaning syrup. In the liberal religious view, even the most self-consciously nihilistic prophets of modernity are misunderstood idealists, affirming what they appear to deny. Schaeffer, on the other hand, can recall why so many modernist movements were, at least in their inception, considered dangerous, as they were meant to be.

In a further paradox, the orthodox evangelical turns out to be a genuine thinker—that is, one who sincerely attempts to understand, in contrast to the more "open-minded" liberals who are only able to reconcile modernity and Biblical faith by not thinking too deeply about either one.

Schaeffer asserts, in *The Church at the End of the Twentieth Century*, that young Christians should not be asked to serve as defenders of the *status quo*, but must be made to understand that Christianity is revolutionary. It is a precept which he follows rigorously in his own work and, once again, it reveals how much more daring he is than liberal religious thinkers who routinely extol accommodations with modern culture.

Liberal religion was born amidst the optimism of the eighteenth century and, although chastened from time to time by disasters like the First World War, it has persisted in that optimism ever since. In order to do so, however, it has been necessary for liberal religious thinkers to contrive to ignore, more and more, all evidences of social and cultural disaster. (Consider, for example, how little contemporary liberal religion has been jolted by the drug culture and the sexual revolution.) Liberals have often been criticized, not least by Schaeffer himself, for compromising Biblical religion in the interests of modern culture. Some liberals come close to acknowledging the charge, while at the same time claiming for themselves a kind of heroic prophecy, a courageous launching out into the unknown.

Often unnoticed even by many of their critics, liberal church members actually derive superficial comfort in the face of the omens and disasters of modern civilization. It allows them to live in relatively untroubled complacency no matter what happens, at the price of subliminally scaling down their religious beliefs to avoid the fierce assaults on those beliefs characteristic of so much of modern culture.

Schaeffer is among the few wide-ranging religious thinkers who has been truly radical in his approach to that culture—in the basic sense of one who is not afraid to diagnose maladies whose roots run deep. Whatever one may think of Schaeffer's diagnoses, they are courageous—not only in that they require an unflinching look at reality; but also in that, if taken seriously, they necessarily induce a sense of anxiety which can only be overcome through faith. Once again, Schaeffer pays modern culture the compliment of taking it seriously, in the way that a physician takes disease seriously.

In one sense, Schaeffer could be described as a true humanist. Although he eschews the term (for Schaeffer humanism is indicative of that which has been responsible for much corruption both in religion and in the world) Schaeffer ultimately is a kind of humanist, in the sense that all Christians must be—that is, because he wishes the best for the human race, and he measures civilization not only by transcendent standards of divine truth, but also by the effects that civilization has on the life of man on earth. Like all authentic Christian thinkers, Schaeffer does not force man to choose between divine duty on the one hand and human fulfillment on the other, but shows how infidelity to the former necessarily undermines the latter. Extending the analogy to the physician, many liberal religious believers can only retain their optimism about modern culture by offering their patients false reassurances about the destructiveness of the diseases which threaten them.

A Question of Roots

Also in *The Church at the End of the Twentieth Century*, Schaeffer makes the distinction between "co-belligerents" and allies in the various struggles against the deformations of modernity. It is a useful distinction, and possibly he would apply it to the relationship between orthodox Roman Catholics and orthodox Protestants at the present time. (He does note in one place that authentic Roman Catholicism is closer to Reformation faith than to modern liberal Protestantism.) In any case, Catholics are likely to find themselves in disagreement with Schaeffer's location of the roots of the modern problem in the theology of Thomas Aquinas.

Because of Aquinas's acceptance of the philosophy of Aristotle, and his systematic attempt to express Christian belief in Aristotelian terms, Schaeffer argues, he introduced into Christianity a view of human reason which made the latter autonomous and ultimately independent of religion. In the century following Aquinas's death this new sense of autonomy was manifest in the Renaissance, which openly espoused the term "humanism." Recognizing that the Renaissance was in no sense an open repudiation of Christianity, Schaeffer argues nonetheless that in thought, and even more tellingly in art, it moved away from the authentic Christian view of man's relationship to God. Ultimately, he thinks, the problem lay in Aquinas's acceptance of the Aristotelian emphasis on the individual object. Once philosophical attention was focused on the individual, Schaeffer believes, it became ultimately impossible to discover a credible universal, in terms of morality or transcendent divine meaning.

There are several debatable elements in this analysis. There is, for example, little evidence that the philosophy of Aquinas had a direct influence on either the art or the thought of the Renaissance, and in some ways the movement known as Humanism was a reaction against the kind of philosophy which Aquinas practiced. Aquinas' "individualism" was known more as a relative thing only—that is, he was a champion of the "universals" against other philosophers who questioned the possibility of knowing them. Finally, it is necessary to question whether intellectual positions, of whatever kind, simply determine what comes afterwards in a uniform way. Most of the time human beings (including philosophers) are not fully logical and hence do not draw inescapable conclusions from their assumptions. Similarly, the nature of cultural change needs to take into account a broad range of factors interacting in different ways under different circumstances.

Nonetheless, orthodox Catholics do have to recognize that the impact of Thomistic philosophy, at least in the past quarter century, has not been altogether healthy. One possible "Thomistic" position is precisely to overemphasize the autonomy of the secular in the way Schaeffer criticizes. This has been particularly evident with respect to ethical questions, where a certain kind of Thomism has tended to approach moral problems in a largely secular spirit, seeking to justify whatever in fact human beings do (for example, with respect to medical technology). But this pattern merely illustrates the fact that ideas do not always have uniform consequences, however, since there are other Thomists who take an opposite position and have struggled energetically and successfully to preserve the claims of the supernatural.

Schaeffer's own position seems in fact to be not as far from Thomism as he seems to think, since he repeatedly emphasizes the necessary unity of faith and intellect—a unity whose sundering he regards as the central misfortune of modern culture. Although Schaeffer believes Aquinas did not succeed in this regard, the maintenance of that unity was clearly one of Aquinas's central concerns—especially in the face of a philosophical movement (often called Latin Averroism) which had already made that disjunction.

Tracing the Decline

Schaeffer's ambitious schema tracing the decline of modern culture is found principally in *How Should We Then Live?*, and recapitulated in several places, notably *The God Who Is There* (for the modern period).

Schaeffer recognizes, as do virtually all contemporary scholars, that it is impossible to interpret the Renaissance, as some earlier writers did, simply as a movement away from religion in favor of a bald assertion of human autonomy. (That interpretation has generally been made by secular admirers of the Renaissance, although it has been employed from time to time by Christian apologists as well.) However, he also realizes that the true significance of a historical period is not always immediately evident. Although it is possible to disagree with some of his interpretations of particular artists and their work, he is no doubt correct to insist that sometimes rather subtle signs suggesting independence from God can be found in the ways in which

Renaissance artists dealt even with religious themes. It is one of the great strengths of Schaeffer's method that he looks not only at the written word but unfailingly at art also, whose messages are sometimes very different, possibly because they are less conscious, from that of the philosophers.

Catholics who disagree with Schaeffer's understanding of the Middle Ages are likely also to disagree at least with some of his emphases with respect to the Reformation (such as his claim that Protestantism consistently opposed all forms of absolute government). Oddly, the Reformation does not claim as much space in Schaeffer's historical analysis as do some other periods. This is because, having situated the beginning of the modern decline in the late medieval period, he is forced to treat the Reformation as something of a parenthesis—opposing the deleterious trends of modernity but ultimately unable to turn them back.

In some ways Schaeffer's own analysis would probably be more forceful if he began it in the seventeenth century, with the birth of modern science. In this way both the late medieval period and the Reformation could be regarded, each in its own way, as dazzling manifestations of a Western Christianity about to decline in cultural importance.

Schaeffer is once again in tune with the best modern scholarship in recognizing that early modern science was not at all hostile to religion but for the most part supported it. Copernicus, Galileo, Bacon, Descartes, Pascal, Kepler, Newton, and numerous others were Christians, and most of them believed that their scientific efforts actually strengthened the foundations of faith rather than weakening them. As Schaeffer points out, their science was not as yet a "closed system." It was still open to God who was outside the system, and they still believed that man too was above the purely material level of existence and could not be accounted for simply in a naturalistic way.

A Radical Break with the Christian Past

It was thus the eighteenth-century Enlightenment which marked the first radical break with the Christian past. Not only was the Enlightenment, to a great extent, overtly and sometimes fanatically anti-Christian; it also asserted the final autonomy of reason and made science into a "closed system." God was retained, in the religion called Deism, but only as an absent divinity with no involvement in the things of earth. Inevitably the Enlightenment carried the seeds of modern utopianism, since the autonomous and closed system of reason was now thought to harbor the possibility of creating a perfect world.

At the heart of Schaeffer's cultural critique is his realization of what is perhaps the central irony of modern civilization—namely, that the grandiose and hubristic claims of reason and of humanity, put forth with increasing confidence, end not in the triumph of rationality, but in virtually the opposite. Modern civilization has been characterized by a seemingly unbridgable gulf between reason and unreason.

The realm of reason has been spectacularly successful if one takes the obvious triumphs of science and technology as its major fruits. But Schaeffer notes that the realm of reason has been, even semiofficially, pessimistic—with scientists and philosophers admittedly unable to provide meaning for existence, no matter how much they pile up rational understandings of the material universe. Indeed, the progress of science—far exceeding what even the most optimistic minds of the eighteenth century foresaw—has been accompanied by a deepening pessimism about human existence which grows directly out of that progress. Since man has been made part of the material world, subject to naturalistic laws and scientific manipulation, he either becomes an absurd being, as Existentialism saw, or his life is simply blotted out in the vast impersonality of nature.

This was seen already in the eighteenth century, by Jean-Jacques Rousseau, whose assertion of absolute freedom was a desperate attempt to retain a sense of the dignity and meaning of human life in the face of this all-devouring materialistic rationalism. With Rousseau began the second half of the modern cultural tragedy. An increasingly irrational assertion of freedom likewise leads to despair and destruction, by unleashing man's hitherto controlled lower powers.

As noted, Schaeffer is not what Catholic theology calls a fidelist—one who merely takes a stand on the subjective rightness of faith. The core of his critique of modern culture is his insistance that authentic human values can be preserved and can flourish only if they rest on some kind of objective basis. Man must know his own nature, must work from the unity of faith and reason which God intended.

Schaeffer sees great significance in the fact that the Marquis de Sade (who can be called the father of modern pornography) was roughly a contemporary of Rousseau as well as an actual participant in some of the events of the French Revolution. Whatever optimism might have been entertained about the likely results of unlimited human freedom, this was already blasted by Sade, who gloried in the perverse uses to which that freedom could be put.

While Immanuel Kant, also a contemporary of Sade, completed the process by which human reason declared itself autonomous (and also, however, admitted its final inability to know reality), it was G.F.W. Hegel, in the next generation, who provided the basis for the modern mode of thought. With his dialectical method there can never be any stable, governing, absolute truth, but only an endless historical process by which ideas modify one another. Schaeffer goes so far as to claim that it is the dialectical method (rather than atheism as such or dogmatic materialism) which is the heart of the Marxist error and its most lethal element. He also points out that, in some form or other, this method has become almost ubiquitous in the modern world—propagated in debased fashion, for example, by the mass media, and unconsciously picked up by ordinary people, including many believing Christians.

Inevitably, the progress of modern theology has not been a fruitful one, given the corruptions of the culture of which it is a part. Schaeffer locates the beginning of this theological decline with the nineteenth-century Lutheran Soren Kierkegaard, who substituted the "leap of faith" for an act of faith in which mind and heart are united. The inevitable outcome of Kierkegaard's move, Schaeffer argues, has been a concept of faith which is purely subjective and without content. One can believe in "god" without being willing to say anything at all about God. Jesus has become, he notes in one place, an "empty banner" on which people can write virtually anything.

The fidelist approach to religion since Kierkegaard is an aspect of the dichotomy which, once again, lies at the heart of modern culture. Reason, man's sole claim to objective knowledge, can induce only pessimism. Whatever optimism man feels about his existence comes from his subjective side. But not only is this subjectivity finally suspect, as wishful self-delusion, it is also the side of man which gives access to his most deformed parts. Modern culture, in its art as well as in much of its thought, is characterized by a spirit of nihilism and despair. The use of drugs is not merely an abberation, but is the inevitable outcome of the modernist agenda. So also is the fashionable flirtation with madness carried on by certain writers. In the end madness and sanity can be securely distinguished only on the basis of an objective theory of personality, which is now lacking, even as madness itself holds a fatal attraction as a perverted kind of absolute.

A Revolutionary Faith

Schaeffer is again perceptive in seeing the significance of the student rebellion of the late 1960s. Because it passed without achieving most of its stated goals, and because many of its participants now look back on their past as a time of youthful folly, it is easy to dismiss it as ephemeral. Schaeffer realizes, however, that it was a direct glimpse into the chaos, despair, and rage which does underlie much of modern culture.

He is again extremely astute in noting that the "swing of the pendulum" back to conservatism is a superficial thing, and in insisting that Christianity does not support the *status quo* but is a revolutionary faith. Given the degeneration and despair of modern culture, a revolution is required to set its values aright. Even the officially orthodox churches are woefully negligent in this regard, he believes.

Given the absence of moral and spiritual absolutes, there are only three alternatives open to civilization, according to Schaeffer—total hedonism, dictatorship by the majority, or a pure dictatorship. Where there are no absolutes society is the only absolute, he observes. Most people, Schaeffer fears, will choose their own unhindered pleasure over freedom, if an absolute state offers them such a bargain.

Although the scourge of liberal religion, Schaeffer has scarcely been an unabashed apologist for the orthodox churches. Despite the common stereotype of the evangelical as merely a defender of conventional values, while the liberal and the radical afflict the comfortable by prophetic speech and action, Schaeffer's upsetting of conventional social arrangements is far more radical than anyone on the Christian left has attempted. For the most part, what the Christian left has done is to assault the fragmentary remains of an older cultural consensus in the name of ideologies which are themselves, as the useful phrase of the 1960s has it, part of the problem rather than the solution. Although talk about "prophecy," "courage," and "truth" flows freely on the religious left, no one there has been able or willing to subject the entire trajectory of modernity to the searching criticisms Schaeffer has mounted.

"Dr. Schaeffer's teaching was for me
like an attractive store which
has behind it a whole warehouse
of good things to be explored."

Richard Winter

Richard Winter (M.B., B.S., L.R.C.P., M.R.C. Psych.)
was a Doctor in Psychiatry at Bristol General Hospital before joining L'Abri Fellowship in England as a staff member. Dr. Winter is the author of *The Roots of Sorrow: Reflections on Depression and Hope* (Marshall and Crossway
Books), and has contributed frequently to medical journals
and Christian publications, with special interest in medical
ethics. He lives with his wife and four children in Greatham,
England.

Near the village church in Huémoz, Switzerland

Chapter Five

The Glory and Ruin of Man

by
Richard Winter
Psychology and Psychiatry

Surgery or psychiatry? That was the difficult choice, between two very different branches of medicine, that faced me after finishing medical school. When, after surgical internships in England and a residency in Canada, I switched my interest to psychiatry, some of my Christian friends were alarmed. At that time Christian psychiatrists were a rare breed. Was it possible to retain one's faith while exploring the chemical and neurological substrata of the mind, and while studying Freud, who thought that religion was just a comforting illusion? Perhaps they also feared for my sanity, and certainly the popular caricature of the psychiatrist almost deterred me! But after seven years of training in psychiatry I was far more convinced of the truth and relevance of Christianity than I had ever been.

I owe much to my parents and my traditional evangelical Christian home, but there was, at that time, little exposure to non-Christian ideas. When I left medical school I started to read much more widely in philosophy and history. In exploring the writings of Sartre and Camus and the other existentialists, I encountered many huge and difficult questions about the existence and nature of God, about reality, and about good and evil. I felt completely overwhelmed with doubt because I was not equipped to answer them. It was then that I remembered that, as

a student, I had struggled through a little book called *Escape
from Reason*. I read it again and then eagerly devoured other
books by Dr. Francis Schaeffer and found, at last, a Christian
who had struggled with the same questions and had discovered
some answers. I then moved to a flying doctor residency with
the Grenfell Association on the Labrador coast. There I shared
some of these new and exciting insights with a very attractive
American girl who was wrestling with similar questions raised
by her studies in English literature. It was not long before she
became a Christian and, six months later, my wife!

Both of us were anxious to learn more; so we returned to
England the long way round the world. As we traveled we read
the sacred scriptures of Buddhism, Hinduism, and Islam and
talked with many people who believed that they had found the
truth about life. We reached Swiss L'Abri far more convinced
that Christianity is the only way to know God and that it is
indeed, as we heard Dr. Schaeffer often say, "true truth" about
the nature of reality. After three months of study at L'Abri
relating the truth of Christianity to philosophy, art, music, and
every other area of life, we returned to England to start my
training in psychiatry.

A Foundation for Understanding

Had I not been so helped by Francis Schaeffer's teaching, I
wonder whether I would have survived psychiatry. In so many
ways he helped me to build a firm foundation and framework
within which to develop a Christian mind in the academic discipline and the therapeutic practice of psychiatry. It was a confidence in that framework of a Biblical view of God and man that
gave me the interest and security in exploring Freud, Jung, the
post-Freudian analysts, Skinner and the behaviorists, Rogers,
Maslow, and the vast range of humanistic ideas and therapies.
My travels in the East, together with Dr. Schaeffer's lectures on
Eastern religion, were very helpful in understanding the powerful emerging influence on transpersonal psychology. I saw, for
the first time, how important world views are in shaping life and
thought. Within this framework I began to learn to discriminate
what was true (to God's reality) and what was false in the

extraordinarily diverse field of psychology and psychiatry. One thing that particularly fascinated me about psychiatry was that, in contrast to surgery, it touched on many other disciplines— law, ethics, philosophy, history, and theology.

In this brief essay I can only outline some of the other important emphases in Dr. Schaeffer's lectures, sermons, and writings that have profoundly influenced my understanding and practice of psychiatry. Always I returned to a simple, yet profound, fact which makes sense of our day-to-day experiential reality—the fact that we are made in the image of the "infinite personal God." We are made with the personal attributes of a loving, creative, thinking, and feeling God so that we may have a living personal relationship with Him. Such personality with all its aspirations does not arise out of "time + chance + nothing"! And because God exists, there is an answer to the question that so many people hardly dare to ask: "What's the point of it all?" We are made to live in a relationship with the God who is really there.

Freedom and Determinism

As I immersed myself in the daily drama of treating disturbed and depressed patients, I also took time to study the history of the development of psychology and psychiatry. Having been forewarned about the subtle and pervasive influence of one's world view, it was not difficult to see how the deterministic and reductionist views of Freud, the behaviorists, and much organic psychiatry led to a dehumanizing picture of man. Dr. Schaeffer did not dismiss the insights of Freud and Skinner completely, but accepted their assertion that we are partially determined. In reflecting on this in his personal correspondence Dr. Schaeffer wrote:

> The Christian position is not that there is no conditioning. There is conditioning of *genetic, sociological* (B.F. Skinner) and *psychological* (Freud) type. The question is whether everything is conditioned. Modern man who sees man only as a machine would say yes; everything is conditioned in one of the three

forms I have mentioned above or a combination of them. The Bible teaches us, and it is the experience of life, that while we are conditioned, yet within the circle of that conditioning there is a self or soul or ego (depending on what discipline we are talking in) that exists that can make choices.. These choices naturally take into account certain factors, but when it is all said and done the important thing is that it is not only a mechanized process. The aspirations of all men and women to feel they are significant in history are not vain and all illusion. We do make choices which do not have a mechanistic previous causality.

You see, the whole thing again always goes back to the presuppositions with which we view the world. For modern man is left with either total causality (in which people are machines) or total chaos. Beginning with the Christian presuppositions you have a very different thing: there is both form and freedom. Thus, while we live in the circle of, let us say, our genetic make-up, yet nevertheless it is possible to have both form and freedom because the individual is made in the image of God and exists. For modern people if all the conditioning were removed there would be nothing there. From the Christian position (and the aspirations of all people) if all the conditioning were peeled away the "I" still exists.[1]

Without God's revelation as the ultimate reference point and framework for truth, non-Christian psychiatrists and psychologists have only their faith in reason and science.

In reaction to the dehumanization of man by the determinists, the humanistic psychologists—strongly influenced by existential and Eastern ideas and anxious to preserve man's uniqueness, dignity, and freedom—rejected Christianity and found their ultimate reference point in personal experience. Carl Rogers wrote, "Experience is for me the highest authority. . . . Neither the revelations of God nor man, can take precedence over my direct experience." For a while, both in America and England, I explored the writings and the therapy groups of the psychological gurus where, it was claimed, self-awareness would lead to growth and self-actualization—to a knowledge of one's inherent goodness and self-perfectibility. These I found to be a strange mixture of true and helpful insights and experiences, but also of many false beliefs about the nature of man and about how to deal with our problems.

The humanistic psychologists are right, of course, to say that man is unique and does have choice and responsibility, and that he is not just determined by his genes and early family experiences. But without God, as John Shotter writes in *Images of Man in Psychological Research,* "man" has to be "a self-defining animal." Abraham Maslow was right to stress our differences from animals (in *Towards the Further Reaches of Human Nature*), and Carl Jung saw the creative potential in the unconscious mind and the imagination. But soon these optimists encountered the limits of their ability to become perfect—in their failure to dislodge real guilt, or to cathartically release anger at the deprivation of early needs, or to cope with existential anxiety about being alone in the universe without God. Many in recent years have turned to some form of transpersonal psychology, finding there a recognition of our spiritual needs, but also a redefinition of reality which in essence says, "you are perfect the way you are"! Thus the *Journal of Humanistic Psychology* now has many articles on Eastern meditation and philosophy.

A Glorious Ruin

As I saw that some schools of psychology and psychiatry dehumanize man and others attempt to deify him, I realized that each was discovering a part of the truth of the diversity of God's creation and redefining the part as the whole. Thus, as Paul says in Romans 1, they were worshiping and serving the creature or part of the creation rather than the Creator. Dr. Schaeffer often spoke of the need for an understanding of the true unity of the world in order to see the place of each aspect of its extraordinary diversity. He also described man as "a glorious ruin"—part glory and part ruin. In Jung and Maslow I saw an attempt to describe something of the glory, and in Freud something of the ruin. Each was attempting to understand the world without acknowledging God or His revelation as the framework and reference point for reality. In another letter Dr. Schaeffer points out the problem with this:

> Psychology and psychiatry must be viewed in two ways. One, beginning with Freud and working on through the usual schools, these men had insights into the bits and pieces of human nature. These bits and pieces are valuable and can be used by the Christian and for the Christian as neutral things because they are true bits and pieces, giving us information about man as he is since the Fall.
>
> The other half of psychology and psychiatric work is these bits and pieces are pushed into the presupposition of natural causes and this in a closed system. Just as naturalistic science against all the basic evidence gets rid of a personal God, so naturalistic psychology against all basic evidences gets rid of man as a personal being.

There is another aspect of Dr. Schaeffer's teaching that is crucial in understanding the complexity of psychological problems, and that is his particular emphasis on "the Fall." I had heard the Fall mentioned vaguely before, but not until my time at L'Abri did I understand its full and momentous significance. Dr. Schaeffer described the result of man's sin ("the Fall"), outlined in Genesis 3, as alienation in four crucial relationships:

> The first alienation was man from God, for which we need salvation through the substitutionary work of Christ. The second alienation is man from himself, which is the psychological alienation. The third alienation is man from other men, which is sociological alienation. The fourth alienation is man from nature and nature from nature, which brings in the problems of ecology. Seeing it this way, we can see that

mental sickness is a result of the abnormality that has
come into the world as a result of the Fall, just as
physical sickness is. And none of us are perfect either
physically or psychologically, but the mix of the Fall
is different in each of us.

Psychology and psychiatry describe the disintegration that we
find at every level of our being and existence. Our minds,
emotions, and wills no longer work as they should; we find we
are divided against ourselves, as Paul found in his own experience—"the good that I would I do not." Our relationships too
become twisted and frustrating. Our sinful nature involves not
only our egocentricity and pride, but the ways we have been
conditioned by the sins of our parents and our culture. Our
bodies are also affected, so that our brain chemistry may be
thrown out of balance by disease or by an inherited predisposi-
tion to depression or anxiety. We *are* partially conditioned, but
we are also responsible for how we react to the sins of our
parents and how we choose to live with our inherited vulnerabilities and disabilities. As I have outlined in my book on depression, *The Roots of Sorrow*, we are all vulnerable to depression in
different ways and some more vulnerable than others.[2] Thus Dr.
Schaeffer wrote to someone who was in despair:

> I would think there are three things about your de-
> spair. First, each of us have slightly different natures,
> and the Fall has left its mark on each of us differently.
> Some have a greater tendency to despondency, and I
> think this is so with you. Secondly, you have had so
> many hurts in the past that you can't expect to get
> over this quickly. However, thirdly (we must face
> this honestly), in the past, and in the more recent
> past, you do do things at times which hurt yourself. I
> pray that these things may grow less and that the Lord
> Himself will gradually heal both your previous hurts
> and your tendency to despondency.

Substantial Healing

In the area of healing, Dr. Schaeffer often spoke of "substantial, but not complete healing this side of glory." He was deeply aware of the struggle and battle against sin and of how much we groan with the whole creation, waiting for the completion of our redemption (Rom. 8:22). And, in psychiatry, I am forced to come to terms with the pain and suffering of a fallen world as I see a few people recover quickly, but many who are caught in desperate vicious circles of their own and others' sin, who need many hours of help.

The more experience I have gained, the more I have become wary of the easy answer, of the cure-all therapy, both in the Christian and non-Christian world. We are all attracted to simple explanations and solutions, but human emotions, thoughts, and behavior cannot be reduced in that way. Dr. Schaeffer, while knowing that many problems are due to sinful actions and attitudes and can be dealt with by repentance, forgiveness, reconciliation etc., also recognized that often it took a long time to help some with deep psychological problems. He saw too that there was real healing in coming to terms with ourselves and our vulnerabilities. "One thing that is helpful," Dr. Schaeffer wrote,

> is learning to live within the limits of who we are. Each of us has our limits in the area of our psychological life, our physical life, and our intellectual life. These limits are set by many things, including the fact that all people have some degree of problems in all these areas as we live in an abnormal world since the Fall. Then too sickness, background, all kinds of things enter in on top of that to set the limits in these areas.
>
> It is very important to learn to live within the limits that we have in all these areas at any given time and to find fulfillment within that relationship rather than beating ourselves to pieces because we do not come up to some idealized and unrealistic standard.

Dr. Schaeffer's teaching was for me like an attractive store which has behind it a whole warehouse of good things to be explored. I found in the philosophical writings of Michael Polanyi and Herman Dooyeweerd a more structured approach to the study of man. Their holistic (and I believe Biblical) view of man demonstrates that each academic discipline deals with only one or two aspects of man's existence and no one aspect can be reduced to any other. The psychiatrist may have to deal with a number of different aspects at once. For instance, the biological aspect in severe depression is treated with antidepressant medication while the psychological aspect of repressed anger and guilt is treated with counseling or psychotherapy. Such therapy may also involve improving communication in the marriage relationship, and practical social, legal, or economic assistance may be needed to clear debts and to find better housing. All of these activities involve working against the effects of the Fall and thus being salt and light in the world. Whether in medicine, psychiatry, or social work we can be ministers of God's "common grace" to a fallen world. At the same time I long to share God's "special grace" in the gospel.

There is a real tension here in trying to help people who do not want to think about God or about the meaning of life. Most just want to get back on their feet again so that they can cope with life. I know that without a relationship with God there can be only very partial healing. Yet, giving a cup of water (or tea!), binding up wounds, weeping with those who weep—Dr. Schaeffer often spoke of the need to feel the pain of this broken world, and in his sensitivity he was not afraid to show his tears—these are an important part of our life, as well as sharing the Good News whenever there is an opportunity. Commenting on one form of psychotherapy, Dr. Schaeffer spoke of this partial healing of the psychological or sociological alienation as a "passing measure":

> Of course it is correct from a Biblical viewpoint that men are alienated on this side of the Fall, and whatever we can do to help cure that alienation is very

helpful. However, from the Biblical viewpoint the central alienation is man's alienation from God. And until this alienation is cured, the psychological alienation of man from himself may be helped slightly, but it is only a passing measure. The same would be true of man's sociological problems [in the alienation] of man from man, and his problem of ecology, in the separation of man from nature.

I feel that all methods of psychology that fall short of this comprehension, while they indeed may be temporarily helpful, cannot touch the central problems.

It was in this area too that I found Dr. Schaeffer's emphasis on the "Lordship of Christ over the whole of life" liberating. No longer did I feel that my whole purpose in life was to evangelize my patients. Yes, I should always be a living witness to the truth, but I could be salt and light in the world whatever I was doing. Whether I was treating a very disturbed psychotic patient with E.C.T., talking with someone about a marriage problem, changing my child's diaper, playing a musical instrument, washing the dishes, planting seeds in the garden, enjoying the beauty of an evening sail, or sharing the gospel with a friend, I should do all in relationship to and for the glory of God. Every part of life is spiritual; being a farmer, carpenter, or psychiatrist is not less spiritual than being a minister or missionary.

Psychology as Religion

Dr. Schaeffer never claimed to have a detailed knowledge of psychology or psychiatry, but he demonstrated a clear understanding of the major underlying philosophical themes. And as I write this essay and read over some of his old letters, I am struck by how much of his framework I have absorbed, only to become consciously aware of its significance months and years later.

He saw that there was a fine line between psychology and theology and was very wary of the tendency of much liberal theology to turn into psychology. Since academic philosophy and liberal theology have admitted they have no real answers to the questions of the meaning of life and have given up the idea of the existence of a personal God, psychology has been thrust into center stage to attempt to provide some practical answers to the man in the street. As one non-Christian psychiatrist has written:

> Many of the people flocking to the growth centres
> . . . the encounter groups . . . seem to us to be un-
> happy, bewildered and disorientated people search-
> ing for some philosophical principle, some system of
> values by which to live. The questions they ask are
> often the ultimate questions concerning existence,
> purpose, the meaning of life, happiness, pain and
> death. Nor is there any doubt that psychotherapists
> are willing to be cast in the role of 'secular pastor
> workers' providing values and meaning of their own.
> Yet we do feel that the announced agenda of psycho-
> therapy, with its heavy medical, secular and pseudo-
> scientific flavour, insufficiently reflects its frankly
> religious undertones.[3]

For this reason many Christians have rejected psychology and psychiatry and believe that all we need is the Bible. There is of course an enormous amount of practical wisdom in the Scriptures that relate to all our day-to-day problems, but I would say with Dr. Schaeffer that psychology is not without value:

> As I see it psychology is a tool. I feel that like other
> tools it can be used or misused. I think, for example,
> that Freud's emphasis on the subconscious, and his
> emphasis that such a thing as guilt feelings do exist
> (in contrast to true guilt) are proper if they are under-
> stood in the Christian framework rather than the
> framework of Freud.
> Of course, Christians should have realized these
> things without Freud's emphasis, but Freud's empha-
> sis has strengthened the matter. I think too that the
> realization that one is affected by one's upbringing
> also has validity and should have been clear without
> Freud.
> Yet, obviously the danger is subtle. The most obvi-

ous danger is that in thinking of the bits and pieces we will tend unconsciously to be infiltrated by some of the naturalistic framework in which almost all psychology as a discipline has been developed.

The Shattered Fragments of Our Lives

As I have struggled, over these years, to integrate psychology and psychiatry within a Biblical Christian framework, it has become increasingly clear that I am in the business of rebuilding the broken fragments of men and women who have been created for something better. As I worked alongside other psychiatrists who had very different views about the nature of man, the image of small groups of soldiers puzzling over pieces of broken eggshell kept returning to my mind. They had never seen Humpty Dumpty before he fell off the wall, and no one knew how the scattered pieces should look when fitted together. Some optimistically pieced a few fragments together while others examined the chemical and physical properties of the shell. A few wise men went off to the King to ask for the original plans so that they could put the pieces together, but most ignored them and struggled on alone. Like these men who ignore the King's original plan of Humpty Dumpty, most psychologists and psychiatrists who examine human behavior have to start with only the pieces they find before them. And with these fragments in hand they have to speculate about the nature of man, where he came from, and where he is going. Their belief about the purpose of life affects the way they help people with problems. So we have today many different schools of therapy, some making grandiose claims about putting man together again, while others more modestly accept that they can do litle more than relieve symptoms and help people to cope a little better with the struggle of a broken life.

It is only as we go to the King and ask for his help and wisdom that we can begin to truly help people to rebuild the shattered fragments of their lives. Although they may discover some healing and help through the practical wisdom of psychology and psychiatry, it is only ultimately in a relationship with God that true integration can be discovered. Psychology and psychiatry carefully sifted and practiced within this framework of truth can then be a powerful tool in helping people who are deeply scarred by "the Fall" and all its consequences, to know again what it means to be made in the image of God and to live in a relationship with the Creator and Lord of the Universe.

"Given his role as a generalist, ... no other modern Christian thinker has attempted such a comprehensive interpretation, and until this happens Schaeffer's work will remain the standard. And, as we have seen ..., the major objections raised against Schaeffer's work simply have not been sustained."

Lane T. Dennis

Lane T. Dennis holds a Ph.D. in the sociology of religion from Northwestern University and an M.Div. from McCormick Theological Seminary, including studies at the University of Basle and the University of Zurich in Switzerland. He is vice president of Crossway Books, and worked closely with Francis Schaeffer in the publication of Schaeffer's last two books. He is the editor of *Letters of Francis A. Schaeffer* (Crossway Books), the author of *A Reason for Hope* (Revell), and a contributor to other books. He lives with his wife and their eight children in Wheaton, Illinois.

Seminar

Chapter Six

Schaeffer and His Critics

by
Lane T. Dennis
Sociology of Religion

An important debate is beginning to take shape among conservative Christians. It has to do with what will be the long-term impact of Francis Schaeffer's thought in relation both to Christianity and to the wider culture.

During his lifetime (1912-1984), Schaeffer wrote twenty-four books, which have sold some three million copies worldwide in more than twenty languages. In his earlier books he demonstrated the philosophic bankruptcy and degeneracy of Western humanistic culture, including the United States, which has abandoned its Judeo-Christian roots and heritage. In his later books, he looked at the natural consequences of this abandonment—rampant secularism, social disintegration, moral degeneracy, sexual perversion, and the deadly consequences of the antilife movement.

Conservative Christians have generally reacted to Schaeffer's thought in either of two ways: (1) they have basically agreed with the "early Schaeffer," but rejected (often rather vehemently) the "later Schaeffer";[1] or (2) they have seen his work as a continuous whole, with the later books flowing naturally out of the positions established in the earlier ones. Since all of the authors contributing to this volume fall generally into this second group, it will not be our purpose here to focus on this view.

101

Instead, in this chapter we will look at some of the criticisms of
this first group (which we shall call "Schaeffer's recent detractors"), to assess their adequacy and accuracy, and to suggest
some reasons why they have reacted in this way.

Rhetoric and Criticism

One cannot read the writings of Schaeffer's recent detractors
without being struck by their rhetorical acrimony. For example,
when contacted by a Christian magazine to review Schaeffer's
major work *How Should We Then Live?* one evangelical leader
declined with the comment that the book is a compilation of "the
most puerile concatenation of unsupported judgments imagin-
able. . . . Schaeffer is . . . making a fool of himself and everyone else who swallows his predigested tripe."[2]

In a review of a later Schaeffer book, which appeared in an
influential Christian magazine, the reviewer describes
Schaeffer's work as "sophomoric bombast," "simplistic," "shal-
low," "tendentious," "muddled," "cruely ironic," "atrophied,"
based on "half-truths . . . more dangerous than falsehoods," and
bordering on "social paranoia."[3] One doesn't usually hear these
kinds of adjectives in polite or scholarly conversation; apparently Schaeffer has touched a raw nerve.

Was Schaeffer a Scholar?

Why such a violent reaction? What nerve was touched? Although there are a number of specific "nerves," there seems to
be a common general criticism to which most of the specific
criticisms are related. In a *Newsweek* article, Professor Mark
Noll of Wheaton College put his finger on it when he observed:
"The danger is that people will take him [Schaeffer] for a scholar, which he is not."[4] This same point of view is widely held
among evangelical academicians.[5] The odd thing is, however,
that at least by normal dictionary definitions, it is incorrect to
say Schaeffer is not a scholar. *The Webster's New World Dictionary*, for example, defines *scholar* as: "1.a) A learned person. b)
A specialist in a particular branch of learning, esp. in the humanities."

We see then that there are two kinds of scholars—the first is "a learned person," and the second is "an academic specialist." Francis Schaeffer was the first type of scholar. There is no question about his learning. He wrote incisively and instructively in areas of theology, art, history, philosophy, ethics, spirituality, and popular culture. Schaeffer was not, however, a scholar in the second sense—that is, he was not an academic specialist, nor did he claim to be. Thus when Noll and others criticize Schaeffer for "not being a scholar," what they apparently mean is that he is not a scholar in this second sense. What is communicated, of course, is that Schaeffer is not a scholar in *any* sense. The effect is that Schaeffer's reputation is inpugned by definitional fiat.

But there is a good deal more at stake here than semantics. If one can discredit one's opponent by *definition*, then one does not need to deal seriously with the opponent's ideas. In the case of Schaeffer, this is exactly what has happened. It works something like this: In the popular mind (and perhaps to an even greater extent in the academic mind) when we say "Joe is a scholar," it carries the strong connotation that "Joe knows what he is talking about." But when we make this statement in the negative—that is, when we say something like "of course, Joe is not a scholar"—the statement carries the strong connotation that Joe does *not* know what he is talking about. This is especially the case when a scholar (i.e., an academic specialist) makes such a statement. In the case of Schaeffer, this method is widely used to imply strongly that "of course, Schaeffer did not know what he was talking about." It's a handy way to win an argument, but does so by definitional imperialism rather than dealing with the real issues.

But the problem goes even deeper than this, for some academic specialists apparently *do* think that Schaeffer doesn't know what he is talking about. Such criticism is most frequently directed at Schaeffer's views in three areas—his views on the "Christian consensus" in early America; his interpretation of the Reformation and its importance; and his reading of the Danish philosopher Søren Kierkegaard (1813-1855). Each of these warrants consideration.

The Myth of Christian America

The first of these criticisms is illustrated well by citing the rest of Noll's quote in *Newsweek*: "The danger is that people will take him for a scholar, which he is not. Evangelical historians are especially bothered by his simplified myth of America's Christian past."[7] Thus, according to Noll, Schaeffer subscribes to a "myth" concerning the influence of Christianity in early America.[8] Of course, there is a kind of "myth of Christian America" which some people do subscribe to, but it is another question as to whether this was Schaeffer's view. The idea actually goes back to the Puritan settlers in early New England. As is widely recognized by historians, the Puritans had a pervasive impact in shaping American cullture.[9] But beyond this, the Puritans viewed themselves as the heirs of the Old Testament covenant with Israel and God's Chosen People in a new land.[10] As for the "myth" today, there probably are some people who believe in the Puritan idea that America is (or was) a "Christian Nation," specially chosen by God as His covenant people in the New World, and that the task we have as Christians is to recover the "Christian Nation" status we once enjoyed.

But is it right to depict Schaeffer as an advocate of the "Christian Nation" idea?[11] Schaeffer does use the terms "Biblical consensus," "Christian consensus," and "Christian ethos" frequently in his writing, and perhaps this is the source of Noll's charge. But if we look at how Schaeffer actually defined these terms we see that he took great care to explain exactly what he meant, and that his definition differs greatly from the "myth of Christian America" and the "Christian Nation" idea. To see this clearly it is necessary to quote at length from Schaeffer as follows:

> The terms "biblical consensus" and "Christian consensus," as used throughout this chapter and the book *[The Great Evangelical Disaster]*, need some clarification. In using these terms I do not mean to say that everyone at the time of the Reformation in Northern

Europe was truly a Christian; nor, when these terms are used in reference to our own country, that everyone in our country was a genuine Christian. Rather this refers to the fact that the Christian world view, and biblical knowledge in particular, were widely disseminated throughout the culture and were a decisive influence in giving shape to the culture. In other words, at the time of the Reformation and in our country up until the last forty to sixty years, the large majority of people believed in basic Christian truths such as: the existence of God; that Jesus was God's Son; that there is an afterlife; that morality is concerned with what truly is right and wrong (as opposed to relative morality); that God is righteous and will punish those who do wrong; that there truly is evil in the world as a result of the fall; and that the Bible truly is God's Word. In the Reformation countries and in our own country up until the last forty to sixty years, most people believed these things—albeit sometimes only in a vague way and often not in the sense that they personally trusted in Christ as their Savior.

Going back to the founding of the United States, this consensus was crucial. This does not mean that it was a golden age, nor that the Founders were personally Christian, nor that those who were Christians were always consistent in their political thinking. But the concept of a Creator and a Christian consensus or ethos was crucial in their work, and the difference between the American Revolution, as compared to the French and Russian Revolutions, cannot be understood without recognizing the significance of the Christian consensus or ethos.

This vast dissemination of biblical knowledge can properly be called a "biblical consensus," a "Christian consensus" or a "Christian ethos." And it may correctly be stated that this "consensus" had a decisive influence in shaping the culture of the Reformation and the extensions of these cultures in North America, Australia, and New Zealand. We must be careful, however, not to overstate the case and imply that the United States ever was a "Christian nation" in a truly biblical sense of what it means to be a Christian, or that the United States could ever properly be called God's "chosen nation."

Moreover, we must acknowledge that there is no "golden age" in the past to which we can return, and that as a nation we have always been far from perfect. As I have mentioned in the past we have had blind spots and serious shortcomings, particularly in three areas: 1) in the area of race; 2) in the area of the compassionate use of wealth— both in how money is made and how money is used; and 3) in wrongly subscribing to the idea of "manifest destiny" as some have done. But having made all of these qualifications, we must nevertheless acknowledge that insofar as the Northern European countries of the Reformation and the extensions of these countries such as the United States do in fact represent a Christian consensus, this consensus has profoundly shaped these cultures, bringing forth many wonderful blessings across the whole spectrum of life. Moreover, the opposite is also true: insofar as our culture has departed from a Christian consensus, as it has so rapidly over the last forty to sixty years, this has had a devastating effect upon human life and culture, bringing with it a sweeping breakdown in morality and in many other ways as well.[12]

One may not agree with every detail of Schaeffer's explanation, but it clearly is a responsible point of view which can be argued convincingly. It is interesting to note, in connection with this, the observations of Alexis de Tocqueville (1805-1859) in his classic work *Democracy in America*, published in 1840.[13] Tocqueville, who was a French social historian and politician and is highly regarded for his perceptive analysis of American society, commented as follows on the influence of religion in America:

> Upon my arrival in the United States, the religious aspect of the country was the first thing that struck my attention; and the longer I stayed there, the more did I perceive the great political consequences resulting from this state of things. . .[14] Christianity . . . reigns without any obstacle, by universal consent. . .[15]
>
> Religion in America takes no direct part in the government of society, but it must nevertheless be regarded as the foremost of political institutions of that country. . . . I do not know whether all Americans have a sincere faith in their religion; for who can search the human heart? But I am certain that they hold it to be indispensable to the maintenance of republican institutions. This is not peculiar to a class of citizens or to a party, but it belongs to the whole nation, and to every rank of society.[16]

Tocqueville, in other words, confirms the same kind of pervasive influence of religion upon the sociopolitical order which Schaeffer identified.[17]

Actually the preceding quote from Schaeffer sets out a rather sophisticated line of argument which reminds one of the thesis of Max Weber (1864-1920), one of the distinguished founders of sociology. As explained in his book *The Protestant Ethic and the Spirit of Capitalism*, Weber's thesis was that the basic ideas of Protestantism, as set forth especially in the Calvinistic tradition, found an economic expression in the rise of capitalism.[18] One of the ways in which he gave support to his theory was to compare the economic development of the Calvinistic-Protestant countries of Northern Europe with the economic development of the non-Protestant countries in Southern and Eastern Europe and also with the Hindu country of India. His conclusion was that the basic ideas of the Calvinistic tradition played a significant role in giving shape to the economic life in the rise of capitalism in Western Europe. It is interesting to note that Schaeffer's thesis directly parallels this—namely, that the "Christian consensus" which grew out of the Reformation left a distinctive mark on the social, political, and economic structures of Western Europe and in particular the United States.[19]

On balance it seems to me that Schaeffer is really making three basic points about America's past which are in the end undeniable: first, that ideas have consequences, and that the "consensus" of ideas at any given time shapes the social, economic, and political order; second, that there were many positive influences which grew out of the "Christian consensus" that largely prevailed (however imperfectly) in the early years of the founding of this country; third, that something has changed drastically over the last forty years or so, resulting in an epidemic of moral perversion of every kind, even to the wanton slaughter of millions of unborn babies. In other words, a cultural revolution has taken place. The decisive influence of a "Christian ethos" has been replaced by an "anti-Christian ethos" of godlessness, immorality, and brutal inhumanity.[20] As Schaeffer stressed often, the answer is not the return to a "mythical golden age" in the past, but to "acknowledge and then act upon the fact that if Christ is our Savior, He is also our Lord in *all* life."[21] To say, then, that Schaeffer is an advocate of the "myth of Christian America," as many of his recent detractors have done, is to propound a view which is not supported by the evidence.

The Golden Age of the Reformation

The second area of major criticism has to do with Schaeffer's views on the Reformation. In this area Schaeffer's recent detractors have argued that he held the position that the Reformation was an era where Christian truth found perfect expression and that it represents a past ideal to which we must return today. For example, Professor Ronald A. Wells summarizes Schaeffer's views on the Reformation as follows:

> Throughout Schaeffer's work is the insistence that modern society . . . should return to the absolute

norms articulated by the Reformation. . . This "Reformation base," it is said, was articulated in Europe and institutionalized (in some large measure) in America. So in Schaeffer's terms, "the base" is "truth" (or, infelicitously, "true Truth"). It is from this base of truth that one measures the shortcomings of modern society. . . . [Thus Schaeffer believes that] if there is not a repository of absolute truths ineradicably fixed in the past, one cannot speak to the present.[22]

Within Wells's summary he makes a number of general assertions about Schaeffer's views. Most important of these, Wells asserts that Schaeffer equated the historical expression of the Reformation with Truth itself—that somehow it was the perfect embodiment of absolute Truth. In addition, he asserts that Schaeffer believed that the Reformation should be our ultimate standard for measuring our society today.

Very similar to this is the criticism of Professor Mark Noll that for Schaeffer

. . .the Reformation era represents a Golden Age from which evangelicals have declined (see *The Great Evangelical Disaster*, p. 118). But surely the elder Schaeffer is mistaken in his frequent assertion that the Reformation preserved both "form and freedom" in perfect balance (*Great Evangelical Disaster*, pp. 21-23).[23]

(In looking up the references in Noll's quote, nothing corresponding to Noll's assertions can be found on these pages.)

What did Schaeffer believe about the Reformation? He did have much appreciation for it, as one would expect any Protestant to have. But did he see it as a "golden age"? Did he want to return to an ideal era in the past? Did he really think that the Reformation had achieved a perfect balance in social and political life? Some of this has been touched on already in the long quote on pages 104-106. But in order to see what Schaeffer actually believed concerning these assertions, it is necessary to quote at length again from Schaeffer's work as follows:

> The Reformation was certainly not a golden age. It was far from perfect, and in many ways it did not act consistently with the Bible's teaching, although the Reformers were trying to make the Bible their standard not only in religion but in all of life. No, it was not a golden age. For example, such overwhelming mistakes were made as Luther's unbalanced position in regard to the peasant wars, and the Reformers showed little zeal for reaching people in other parts of the world with the Christian message. Yet though they indeed had many and serious weaknesses, in regard to religious and secular humanism, they did return to the Bible's instruction and the example of the early church. . . .[24]
>
> [Concerning] the political freedom which the return to biblical Christianity gradually brought forth . . . The accent here is on the word *gradually*, for all the results did not come at once. Let us emphasize again that the Reformation was no golden age; and our eyes should not turn back to it as if it were to be our perfect model. People have never carried out the biblical teaching perfectly. Nonetheless, wherever the biblical teaching has gone, even though it has always been marred by men, it not only has told of an open approach to God through the work of Christ, but also has brought peripheral results in society, including political institutions. . . .
>
> The Reformation did not bring social or political perfection, but it did gradually bring forth a vast and unique improvement. . . .[25]

Similarly, I would repeat part of the quote cited earlier from *The Great Evangelical Disaster*:

Moreover, we must acknowledge that there is no "golden age" in the past to which we can return, and that as a nation we have always been far from perfect. As I have mentioned in the past we have had blind spots and serious shortcomings, particularly in three areas: 1) in the area of race; 2) in the area of the compassionate use of wealth—both in how money is made and how money is used; and 3) in wrongly subscribing to the idea of "manifest destiny" as some have done. But having made all of these qualifications, we must nevertheless acknowledge that insofar as the Northern European countries of the Reformation and the extensions of these countries such as the United States do in fact represent a Christian consensus, this consensus has profoundly shaped these cultures, bringing forth many wonderful blessings across the whole spectrum of life. . . .[26]

As in the case of "the myth of Christian America" we also see that the assertions made by Wells and Noll are simply unfounded.[27]

But it is interesting to consider further what Wells's own views of the Reformation are, as presented, for example, in his critique of Schaeffer. Thus Wells explains:

. . . So, what is my critique of Schaeffer? His confusion rests on his inability to see Protestantism as the religious form of Renaissance humanism. To be sure, Protestants *said* that their consciences were informed by the Bible, on which authority alone rests ("*sola scriptura*"). Yet we all know of Protestant inability to agree on what the Bible said, or even on what kind of book it is.

In his triumphalism, Schaeffer cannot see the ironic and tragic in the Protestant movement, because he refuses to see it as an aspect of the humanist movement itself. In his various works Schaeffer repeatedly invokes the Reformation as the answer to

the problem of humanism, when in reality it is part of
the problem.[28]

Actually Wells holds a rather novel view of the Reformation—that it was "really" an epiphenomenon of Renaissance
humanism. This view may be gaining strength among secular
historians who, of course, would like to find nonreligious, re-
ductionistic explanations for all religious phenomena. But it is
hardly the view of the classic historians of the Reformation such
as Roland Bainton and Jaroslav Pelikan. I would think Martin
Luther (1483-1546) would also find it surprising to learn that his
agony over his personal salvation was really a "religious form of
Renaissance humanism." To be sure, the whole cultural milieu
needs to be taken into account when considering the Reformation; Christianity never exists in a vacuum. But Wells's view
clearly does not take sufficient account of the *distinctive* way in
which the Reformation interacted with Renaissance humanism.
Moreover, Schaeffer was quite aware of the issue and showed
considerable balance in handling it. Thus Schaeffer wrote:

> The men of the Reformation did learn from the new
> knowledge and attitudes brought forth by the Renais-
> sance. A critical outlook, for example, toward what
> had previously been accepted without question was
> helpful. . . . But from the critical attitude toward the
> traditions which had been accepted without question,
> the Reformers turned not to man as beginning only
> from himself, but to the original Christianity of the
> Bible and the early church. Gradually they came to
> see that the church founded by Christ had since been
> marred by distortions. However, in contrast to the
> Renaissance humanists, they refused to accept the
> autonomy of human reason, which acts as though the
> human mind is infinite, with all knowledge within its
> realm. Rather, they took seriously the Bible's own
> claim for itself—that it is the only final authority.[29]

For Schaeffer, the Reformation—with all its imperfections, but at the same time with its clear emphasis on the Bible alone, justification by grace through faith, and the priesthood of all believers—was a source of inspiration. Wells is apparently uncomfortable with this source, and in its place he offers his own sources. Among these he first singles out Walter Rauschenbusch (1861-1918), the "father of the social gospel"—a man who "had no room in his theology for the substitutionary atonement, a literal hell, or a literal second coming." He was also a Socialist who called for the collective ownership of property, and held nearly utopian views of human potential.[30] The second person Wells mentions is Reinhold Niebuhr (1892-1971), the neoorthodox theologian and ethicist about whom the *Oxford Dictionary of the Christian Church* states: "the theology of the Creeds in its traditional form he rejects as spurious metaphysics which reduces true Christian faith to logical nonsense."[31]

With Rauschenbusch and Niebuhr among his primary sources, Wells goes on to set out his agenda for Christian cultural interaction. "But whatever our stand is or ought to be," Wells writes, "it must include the following:"

> (1) *Definitive repentance from Protestant triumphalism* . . . not depending on a sectarian view of history, especially of the Reformation. (2) *Definitive repentance from association with American cultural religion.* . . . (3) *Definitive repentance from the "evangelical ethos.".* . .[32]

Number two sounds fine; Schaeffer never liked cultural religion anyway. But numbers one and three? We are apparently supposed to *repent* (i.e., to abhor and turn from) our own Christian convictions as evangelical Protestants.

In summarizing Wells's critique of Schaeffer on the Reformation, then, we find that Wells's presentation of Schaeffer's views is simply wrong;[33] that Wells's own views are novel and at best dubious; and that his solution is apparently nonevangelical as regards his primary sources and his agenda for a remedy.[34]

Revering Kierkegaard

The third area of major criticism of Schaeffer has to do with his treatment of certain major thinkers of the past. Probably the best example of this are those who have criticized Schaeffer for his views on Søren Kierkegaard (1813-1855). We need not go into this as extensively as in the case of the other two criticisms, since Kierkegaard is also discussed in Chapter Three of this book, and since we do not have the space available to handle this in a comprehensive way. But even a brief analysis is instructive.

In recent years there has been a growing appreciation for Kierkegaard among evangelicals. For example, C. Stephen Evans, a former Wheaton College professor who is currently associate professor of philosophy at Saint Olaf College, writes:

> Strangely, almost the only group that does not admire and revere Kierkegaard is the one group with whom I believe he had the strongest degree of spiritual kinship: evangelical Christians. More than once I have been asked by evangelicals whether or not Kierkegaard was a Christian. More than once I have seen shocked faces when I expressed my opinion that Kierkegaard is a great resource for Christian philosophers, theologians, and psychologists. Why should this be so?
>
> The answer is complicated, and is probably best left to the historian. But at least one section of the complicated answer is that some well-known evangelical pastors and authors have chosen Kierkegaard as a central villain in their account of how the twentieth century lost its faith and its moorings.[35]

Evans goes on to identify Francis Schaeffer as the primary cause for the vilification of Kierkegaard.

From this we see that Evans thinks that we should admire and even revere Kierkegaard and that Schaeffer apparently has a very distorted view of him. Others have echoed this later assertion, claiming that Schaeffer's view is "simplistic,"[36] and that it doesn't even correspond to the general descriptions offered in the standard textbooks and reference works.[37] In view of these charges, it would be instructive once again to see what Schaeffer actually does say about Kierkegaard and to see whether his views are credible.

> It is often said that Søren Kierkegaard, the Dane (1813-55), is the father of all modern thinking. And so he is. He is the father of modern existential thinking, both secular and theological thinking. . . .
>
> Why is it that Kierkegaard can so aptly be thought of as the father of both? What proposition did he add to the flow of thought that made the difference? Kierkegaard led to the conclusion that you could not arrive at synthesis by reason. Instead, you achieve everything of real importance by a leap of faith.
>
> Kierkegaard was a complex man and his writings, especially his devotional writings, are often very helpful. For example, the Bible-believing Christians in Denmark still use these devotional writings. We can also be totally sympathetic to his outcry about the deadness of much of the Church in his day. However, in his more philosophical writings he did become the father of modern thought. This turns upon his writings of Abraham and the "sacrifice" of Isaac. Kierkegaard said this was an act of faith with nothing rational to base it upon or to which to relate it. Out of this came the modern concept of a "leap of faith" and the total separation of the rational and faith. . . .
>
> I do not think that Kierkegaard would be happy, or would agree, with that which had developed from his thinking in either secular or religious existentialism. But what he wrote gradually led to the absolute separation of the rational and logical from faith.[38]

Is this an incredulous view? Not at all; it seems rather to strike a careful balance. On one hand, Schaeffer points out the positive contribution of Kierkegaard in his devotional writings and in his critique of spiritual deadness in the church. On the other hand he sees a serious problem in Kierkegaard's thought on the relationship between reason and faith, and also insofar as his thought led to secular and religious existentialism.

But is Schaeffer right concerning the problem of faith and reason in Kierkegaard? Scholarly opinion is currently divided on this,[39] and it appears unlikely that there ever will be a consensus in either direction.[40] All the same there are a number of philosophers, such as Brand Blanshard at Yale, who have understood Kierkegaard in ways very similar to Schaeffer.[41] As for the existential legacy of Kierkegaard, this view is supported without exception in the standard reference works.[42]

In briefly considering Schaeffer's views on Kierkegaard, then, what we find is not unlike the other two criticisms— namely, that Schaeffer's views are misrepresented, and that an alternate, somewhat novel view is being advanced by his critics. It is useful to compare Schaeffer's attempt at striking a careful balance with Evans's statement about revering Kierkegaard;[42] it is also notable that some twenty years after Kierkegaard's influence among religious liberals has waned, he is now being rediscovered by evangelicals.

A Pattern of Criticism

In concluding our survey of the three areas where Schaeffer had been criticized most often, we see a pattern developing in the way Schaeffer's recent detractors have handled his work as follows: (1) a basic criticism is made of Schaeffer's work in a particular area; (2) Schaeffer's view in this area is then presented in a way which is substantially false; (3) the false understanding of Schaeffer's view is then shown by Schaeffer's critic to be "untenable"; (4) the critic then presents his own "tenable" view; (5) upon inspection, however, it is the critic's "tenable" view (not Schaeffer's "untenable" view) which turns out to be seriously defective. This is not to say that Schaeffer's views are beyond dispute. The point is simply that they deserve to be handled in a responsible manner, especially by those who are academic specialists. Finally, although we have considered only three major areas of objection to Schaeffer's thought, the same pattern can be seen in many other critiques of his work. (See pages 231-234, note 44, for additional examples of this same problem.)

What Was Francis Schaeffer?

Although we have found that the three major objections to Schaeffer described above cannot be sustained, it still remains to put this into clearer perspective. Why should there be such an intense reaction to Schaeffer, even when it is unfounded? I would suggest that this can be answered best by considering *what* Schaeffer was and how this relates to his recent detractors.

What was Francis Schaeffer? Was he a scholar? Was he primarily an evangelist? Was he something else in addition to these? At the beginning of this chapter we saw that he was indeed a scholar—in the first sense of being a remarkably learned man, but not in the second sense of being an academic specialist. Much of the tension between Schaeffer and his opponents arises out of the difference in these two definitions of scholar. But the tension is heightened by two additional factors. The first of these has to do with Schaeffer's own self-understanding that his primary calling was that of an evangelist. In fact this became such an important issue for Schaeffer that he wrote a new appendix to *The God Who Is There* in 1981 on "The Question of Apologetics." As Schaeffer explained:

> People often say, "What are you?" and I at times have said, "Well, basically I am an evangelist." But sometimes I do not think people have understood that does not mean that I think of an evangelist in contrast to dealing with philosophic, intellectual or cultural questions with care.
>
> I am not a professional, academic philosopher— that is not my calling, and I am glad I have the calling I have, and I am equally glad some other people have the other calling. But when I say I am an evangelist, it is not that I am thinking that my philosophy, etc. is not valid—I think it is. . . . That is not to say that all my answers are correct. Nor is it to say that the more

academically oriented philosopher cannot deal with
more of the necessary details. But what I am saying is
that all the cultural, intellectual or philosophic material is not to be separated from leading people to
Christ. I think my talking about metaphysics, morals
and epistemology to certain individuals is a part of
my evangelism just as much as when I get to the
moment to show them that they are morally guilty
and tell them that Christ died for them on the cross. I
do not see or feel a dichotomy: *this* is my philosophy
and *that* is my evangelism. The whole thing is evangelism to the people who are caught in the second
lostness we spoke of—the second lostness being that
they do not have any answers to the questions of
meaning, purpose, and so on. . . .

There certainly is a place for a study of philosophy
as a scholarly discipline in great detail. That too can
be a Christian's calling. But if the total course does
not give answers so that the students are left with
more than probability in regard to Christianity, it is
much less than a course in philosophy can and should
be.

To me there is a unity of all reality, and we can
either say that every field of study is a part of evangelism (especially useful to certain people in the
world); or we can say that there is no true evangelism
that does not touch all of reality and all of life.[45]

Thus Schaeffer does not claim to be an academic specialist (in
history, or philosophy, or any other discipline), and he emphasizes the need for specialists to undertake in-depth work in each
of these fields. But he also emphasizes the unity of all reality and
the need for evangelism to touch every area of life with valid
answers. At this point, we can again see the tension insofar as
some have taken Schaeffer's calling as an evangelist to mean
that he could not therefore know what he was talking about.
There is no intrinsic reason why this should be true, and of

course Schaeffer believed his answers were valid. What we see here is the same kind of problem mentioned at the beginning of the chapter concerning the definition of scholar. The validity of Schaeffer's work needs to be determined on its own merit, not dismissed by definitional fiat.

But in addition to being a scholar (i.e., a learned person), and an evangelist, Schaeffer was also something else—namely a *generalist*. As a generalist, a further kind of tension exists between Schaeffer's work and the work of the academic specialist. The specialist is interested primarily in a comprehensive, in-depth understanding of a specific discipline, while the generalist is interested primarily in understanding the interrelationship of various disciplines. Or to use Schaeffer's terms, the specialist is concerned with the particulars; the generalist is concerned with universals. We live, however, in an age of specialization, when the dominant world view denies the reality of universals altogether. Consequently, there is a natural tendency to dismiss the work of the generalist out of hand. Schaeffer says, however, that universals not only exist, but that we can *know* these in a personal way; and further, that we cannot properly understand the particulars unless we have some understanding of the universals. Or to put it another way, the knowledge of facts (the particulars) in a specific discipline is of little value unless it can be related in a meaningful way to the whole of life (the universals).

The work of the specialist and of the generalist, then, need to be seen as complementary rather than as contradictory. For in understanding the unity of reality (i.e., the interrelationship of the particulars), the *generalist* also needs to have specific understanding of the various particular fields of knowledge. And in order for the *specialist* to understand the meaning and significance of even his own particular specialty, he also needs to have a broad understanding across the full spectrum of knowledge. Although Schaeffer (the generalist) recognizes the legitimacy of the specialist's work, the compliment, unfortunately, is seldom returned. Why is this? Much of the objection to Schaeffer's work is simply the result of basic differences between specialists and generalists, both in methods and goals, and of the reluctance of many specialists to grant any legitimacy at all to the generalist's work.

Thin Ice and the Generalist

As one of Schaeffer's reviewers observed, the work of the generalist "is the thinnest of thin ice [and] anyone who does it courts disaster."[46] There are indeed dangers in being a generalist. There is the danger, first, of oversimplification—although simplification is a necessary part of the generalist's work. The generalist is trying to provide an overview, or a general map of the terrain, which shows the interrelationship of various areas. Without a general map, it is impossible to know where one is and how the various areas relate to each other. The general map of course will need to be supplemented by specialized maps of much more detail. Thus Schaeffer emphasized that "there certainly is a place for a study of philosophy [or any other field] as a scholarly discipline in great detail. That too can be a Christian's calling."[47] Schaeffer's concern, however, was that philosophy, or any other discipline, needs to go beyond mastery of the details and to see the relationship of each discipline to the general map—to the larger questions of meaning, purpose, and the unity of all reality. Without this, the study of details is meaningless.

Another danger is the danger of mistakes in the details. Schaeffer was aware that "not . . . all my answers are correct,"[48] and in response to criticism over certain details Schaeffer once wrote:

> I think the best thing to do is to divide my answer into two levels:
> 1. Of course one wants to be totally accurate historically and I am very much open to have detailed mistakes, whether in history or other fields, pointed out and to be rectified in future works. . . . I assure you that I am interested in historical accuracy.
> 2. There is another element involved, however, in many of these discussions. That is that detail is used not for increased accuracy but in order to undermine

the whole direction of what is involved in the book's
major thesis rather than the detail.[49]

Schaeffer's concern was that, in the battle for Christian Truth,
his opponents would distort the significance of a minor error in
detail so as to undermine the battle.

Within Schaeffer's work there are of course errors of detail,
and there will always be differences of interpretation—as in the
case of anyone's work. But, given his role as a generalist, he is
in fact remarkably accurate in the handling of a vast range of
knowledge—from art to ecology, from pop music to philosophy,
from law to literature. Schaeffer's analysis and interpretation of
Western culture surpasses the work of Lord Kenneth Clark (*Ci-
vilisation*), and by far the work of Jacob Bronowski (*The Ascent
of Man*), in both fairness and insight. No other modern Christian
thinker has attempted such a comprehensive interpretation, and
until this happens Schaeffer's work will remain the standard.[50]
And, as we have seen above, the major objections raised against
Schaeffer's work simply have not been sustained.

But a further danger grows out of the positive contribution
Schaeffer has made—that is, because Schaeffer has been so
successful as a generalist some have used his work as a substitute for doing the in-depth study of a specialist. An example of
this would be the college student who quotes Schaeffer's conclusions as an appeal to a final authority, rather than doing the
research himself and supporting his conclusions from primary
sources. This misuse of Schaeffer's work is surely one of the
major frustrations of those academic specialists who have ob-
jected to Schaeffer. Instead of this approach, those who have
been influenced by Schaeffer could perhaps make a major contribution by doing the comprehensive work of a specialist in
various disciplines in light of what they have learned from their
mentor.

Thin Ice and the Specialist

But if the generalist has to skate on thin ice, so also does the
specialist. And the dangers of being a specialist, in an age when
specialization is revered, may be even more critical. In becom-

ing a specialist, one must immerse oneself in a world of ideas which is in direct conflict with the Christian world view. As C. S. Lewis observed in his essay "Christianity and Culture": "There is no neutral ground in the universe: every square inch, every split second, is claimed by God and counterclaimed by Satan."[51] And there is no place where the battle rages more intently than in the universities where one becomes certified as a specialist. It is not easy to go through a Ph.D. program without being affected by the naturalistic presuppositions which reign virtually unchallenged in every discipline. It is not easy to write one's doctoral dissertation without giving assent to some form of reductionism. There is a fundamental conflict between the Christian point of view and the non-Christian point of view. The non-Christian thinks that the supernatural categories of the Christian are absurd, and that man and all of reality can be explained in naturalistic terms. The danger is that in being forced to play the game by the naturalist's rules, we will eventually absorb some form of naturalism ourselves and abandon a distinctively Christian position. I remember talking with a Christian psychology professor, saying how hard it was to "do" sociology (my discipline) without resorting to some form of naturalistic explanation. His response was that when it comes to doing psychology as an academic discipline, we have to of course assume a naturalistic methodology.

This kind of response, which is all too common among Christian academic specialists, and which cedes the battle to the naturalist and materialist before the first shot is even fired, is the exact kind of thing Schaeffer would not allow in his own work. Schaeffer's unwillingness to accommodate Christianity to anti-Christian premises in academic disciplines is also what got him into trouble with the Christian academic specialists. But it is the only way to preserve the integrity of Christianity when confronted with the corrosive assumptions of modern thought.

Are we willing, in each of our academic fields, to show the deficiencies of the naturalistic assumptions, as they distort our explanations of man and the world? Are we willing to stand at the point where the battle rages? If not, we have been lost for the battle and our skills as specialists are without real value.

A related danger is the tendency to adopt a kind of style which emphasizes only give-and-take, dialogue, openness, and intellectual detachment, but which is unwilling to take a stand or speak the truth boldly especially when it may be painful. Here I am reminded of Schaeffer's illustration of "taking the roof off." As Schaeffer explains, the modern man who is not a Christian must build an intellectual shelter or "roof" over his head "as a protection against the blows of the real world."[52] Until this roof or false world view is removed, the person will be unable to hear and understand the gospel, and will continue to live without ultimate meaning in life. "The Christian," Schaeffer writes,

> lovingly, must remove the shelter and allow the truth of the external world and of what man is, to beat upon him. When the roof is off, each man must stand naked and wounded before the truth of what is. . . .
>
> It is unpleasant [to have reality come crashing down upon us], but we must allow the person to undergo this experience so that he may realize his system has no answer to the crucial questions of life.[53]

Schaeffer explains that until the protection of the false world view is removed, the gospel will seem like nonsense.

> Hell or any such concept is unthinkable to modern man because he has been brainwashed into accepting the monolithic belief of naturalism which surrounds him. . . .
>
> Hence we begin to deal with "modern man" by preaching at the place he can understand. Often he understands the horrible point of meaninglessness. Often he recognizes the tension between the real world and the logic of presuppositions. Often he appreciates the horror of being dead and yet still alive. . . .
>
> This is what we mean by taking the roof off. But we cannot ever think this to be easy.[54]

The danger here is that in our give-and-take, openness, dialogue and intellectual detachment we will not be willing to lovingly "take the roof off," especially at the point where we as Christians stand in direct conflict with the naturalistic assumptions of our colleagues.

A final danger is the tendency to elevate one's specialty till it becomes an intellectual path for achieving spiritual enlightenment. The specialist, however, has no special insight into other fields outside of his discipline; nor does he have greater spiritual wisdom, or greater ethical judgment by virtue of being a specialist. As C. S. Lewis wrote, concerning the relationship of his own expertise in literature to spiritual and ethical matters:

> In the judgements of beliefs . . . we humbly hope that we are being trained, like everyone else, by reason and ripening experience, under the guidance of the Holy Ghost, as long as we live, but we speak on them simply as men, on a level with all . . . [other] Christians, and indeed with less authority than any illiterate man who happens to be older, wiser, and purer, than we.[55,56]

As Long as We Live

C. S. Lewis's description of a man trained by reason and ripening experience, under the guidance of the Holy Spirit, to the end of his life, seems a fitting description of Francis Schaeffer. With his reason he struggled with the great intellectual and theological questions of the day, finding the only sufficient answers in the written Word of God. As a man of experience he sought to know and understand every area of life and culture, but just as much to understand the experience of modern man—lost in hopelessness and despair—and to pour his life out in reaching the spiritual and physical needs of all whom the Lord brought to his doorstep. As a man under the guidance of the Holy Spirit, he sought to live day by day, moment by moment, in communion with his Lord and Savior, and in bearing witness to the Lordship of Christ across the whole spectrum of life. All these things he sought to carry out to the end of his life.

As mentioned at the beginning of the chapter, there are those who are unhappy about, even embarrassed by, Schaeffer's activism in the closing years of his life—who saw this as a basic departure from his earlier commitments. But Schaeffer did not see it this way, especially in relation to the question of abortion. Abortion was the logical, deadly consequence of the same philosophical, moral, and spiritual issues he had dealt with for decades. No genuine distinction can be made between the intellectual concerns of the "early Schaeffer" and the activist concerns of the "later Schaeffer." It is true that, after the *Roe v. Wade* decision in 1973, our land became drenched in the blood of the innocent unborn, and the fight for life was raised to a critical level calling for urgent new strategies. But the fight for life was nothing new to Francis and Edith Schaeffer. Their home had already been a shelter for many unwed mothers and other casualties of modern life, decades before *Roe v. Wade.*

There was nothing most consistent than for Francis Schaeffer to wage the battle on this front with his last strength. Schaeffer was diagnosed as having lymphoma cancer in 1978, just after completing the film series *Whatever Happened to the Human Race?* And though he was in and out of the hospital for the last six years of his life, he often said that the Lord had graciously made these his most productive years. But many lose sight of the fact that he was a very sick man during this time. He often confessed to me, as he did to many others, that he didn't think he could climb the mountain one more time.

The last six months of Schaeffer's life could best be described as a daily struggle against death—in the form of the cancer which was claiming his own body, but just as much a struggle against the spiritual and moral death which was claiming the lives of individuals and of our society as a whole. In December of 1983 he was flown unconscious to Mayo Clinic and not expected to live more than a few days. (A few weeks earlier he had marched on the picket lines in front of a hospital to protest the abortions being committed inside.) But Schaeffer still had one more battle to fight—a book to complete, a nationwide seminar tour to ten Christian colleges. By the middle of January he had regained enough strength to undergo a life-extending operation, and to complete work on the book. But by the middle of February he had slipped into serious condition again and it seemed impossible that he would be able to go on the tour. Complications were setting in, his veins had collapsed from months of IVs and injections, and he needed another operation to implant a tube in his chest so that his daily medication and future transfusions could be put directly into his system.

Schaeffer did not have to climb the mountain this one last time, but it was his hope to do so which kept him alive in the closing months of his life. On March 1, 1984 he was given an extra transfusion and flew to Virginia for the first seminar. During the next seven weeks he traveled from hotel to hotel across the country, getting out of his bed only to handle his part of the program at each college. Sustained literally by the prayers of thousands of Christians, Schaeffer completed the tour, and his last battle for the physical and spiritual lives of others. Through Christ his Lord, he won the battle on May 15, 1984. Through Christ our Lord, the battle remains for each of us to carry on.

Part Two

THE PRACTICE
OF TRUTH

"I saw so many people changed at L'Abri. Many became Christians; some did not. But I think that most went away with the knowledge that they had been loved—with a sense of worth and a clear idea of the existence of God."

Maria Walford-Dellù

Maria Walford-Dellù, a linguist, frequently translated Dr. Schaeffer's lectures into Italian and French, both at L'Abri in Switzerland and during seminars in Italy. Born and raised in Italy, she has also lived in Switzerland, England, Holland and the U.S.A. She received the *Licence es Lettres* from the University of Lausanne (Switzerland), and pursued post-graduate studies at the Free University of Amsterdam (Holland). She is currently preparing for a Ph.D. in Italian Literature from the University of Chicago. She lives with her husband and their three children in Wheaton, Illinois.

Francis and Edith Schaeffer

Chapter Seven

You Can Have a Family with Us

by

Maria Walford-Dellù
Personal Ministry

It is always difficult to find words to describe an important moment of life, an intense feeling, or a person dearly loved. Being faced now with the challenge of giving a portrait of Dr. Schaeffer, a man whose life touched mine deeply, feelings of gladness are mixed with a sense of how disappointing a mediocre portrait can be, reflecting the failures of the one who has made it and not the rich complexities of the one depicted.

I remember vividly my first meeting with Dr. Schaeffer—in 1962 as I recall—when I was still living in my home city of Milan, Italy. My pastor, Hurvey Woodson, invited me to a Bible study which Schaeffer was going to lead. Hurvey and his wife, Dorothy, were the L'Abri workers in Italy and had helped nurture my new faith in the little group of believers meeting in their home. But for some months I had rarely been able to attend such meetings. Although I had a deep desire to be with Christian people, my parents forbade me to read the Bible or to talk to anybody about my newfound faith. Sincere Roman Catholics, my parents were raised at a time when people were not allowed to read the Scriptures, since the Church wanted to be the sole source of instruction in order to avoid heresy.

I had been fortunate, however, to go to Cambridge, England, at the age of nineteen to refine my English. It was there that I first met people who studied the Bible. Before long I came to faith in Christ in a most remarkable way, which was itself evidence of God's existence. When I returned to Italy, my parents were disappointed and distressed, and tried to protect me by forbidding anything that might nourish my new ideas. Hurvey Woodson's words of respect for Dr. Schaeffer, however, prompted me to take up his invitation despite the personal consequences at home.

At the end of that evening, Dr. Schaeffer asked me to tell him frankly about my situation at home. He listened carefully and then said, "Maria, if one day you have to leave home, you know that you can have a family with us."

I was very upset by these words. He did not know how much my family loved me and I loved them. That would never happen to me! But it did. When forced to choose between them and my Christian faith, I left home. In the midst of this conflict, I found comfort in Dr. Schaeffer's words.

L'Abri as a Family

Since Schaeffer had offered L'Abri as a second home for me, I moved to Switzerland and enrolled at the University of Lausanne, which was an hour and a half away from the Schaeffers' home in Huémoz. For the next seven years I went up to L'Abri almost every weekend and every other time I was free from my studies and my job. When the numbers at L'Abri increased, there was always a place for me, even if I could sleep only on the floor.

At the beginning, life in Lausanne was difficult. Separation from my family was hard; I felt empty without their love and without the friendship of my brother. I was missing them as well as my numerous cousins, uncles, and aunts with whom I had had such a close contact all my life. Having been asked by my parents to leave home, although they loved me and I understood their reasons, I was left insecure and wondering, "Will I be able to be loved again, and if so will love be lasting in this world?" God knew my questions; and even though I had not expressed them, he used the Schaeffers to bring stability and love back into my life.

I remember vividly the feeling of well-being which enveloped me during those visits—the warm welcome as I went into the kitchen without having to ring the bell before entering the house. Mrs. Schaeffer was usually there—cooking away, having at least five ideas at a time about the different meals to be prepared for the weekend. Her meals were a feast for the eye, and she always had something interesting to say about God and the people that He had sent there. All this was intermingled with explanations about the food she was preparing, its size, shape, color, and nutritional value. She would answer the serious questions of the girls who were working with her, watch that they were carefully doing what was needed, answer the telephone, keep an eye on Franky, and go to see Dr. Schaeffer when he called loudly down the stairs, "Edith! Edith!" Besides all this, she would see that nothing was burning in the oven, arrange flowers, fix a cup of tea for the newcomers.

I always enjoyed helping out with the work in those first years before so many people started coming. My task was usually to prepare the salad, and whatever else was necessary, while trying to listen and to take delight as much as possible in the close company of the people working there.

Mrs. Schaeffer considered her home as a center for creativity. Many examples and ideas, which I saw demonstrated firsthand in her kitchen, were later developed in her books. The preparation of a meal was a ceremony which conveyed a sense of marvel and joy to me and to many others.

During those Saturday afternoon sessions in the kitchen, Dr. Schaeffer would dash down the stairs—he never came up or down slowly or quietly. He would come to greet me saying, "Welcome back, it must be another weekend. It seemed only yesterday that you left. I knew that you were here; I heard your laughter." The way his eyes lit up, and the tone of his voice, reminded me, each time, of the genuine affection that he felt for me, as he did for many others like me. He would ask me how I was and then made sure that we would have some time to talk and pray together before I left again for Lausanne.

Dr. Schaeffer never dwelt on preliminaries; he went right to what was important. He showed concern and understanding, always encouraging me to obey God and to do His will. He was very pleased when I would do well in my studies and always encouraged me to go further. I was so glad that he wanted to spend time with me, especially since his life was very busy. They were moments to look forward to, and moments of truth. I thought, as I was sitting there, of all those others who went to pray and talk with him. He had a way of looking into one's eyes for a few seconds, concentrating on you alone at that moment to the exclusion of all else. These times were very precious.

With every room in their home in use, the Schaeffers' bedroom became his study and place to meet with people. Soon the content of that room became very familiar to me—with his books spread on the bed and his rocking chair right beside it. We prayed for each other, for our families, for the work of L'Abri. He always remembered Italy, especially Milan which he felt was spiritually a very dark city. As I was there my eyes scanned round the room, noting among his books one about Leonardo and another about Michelangelo. It pleased me to see that he appreciated their art although he did not agree with their philosophy.

I could never go in that room without thinking of the life of sacrifice that the Schaeffers were leading. They were sharing their home, their food, their records; they were giving generously of all that they had, their possessions and their energy. Indeed it was a life of sacrifice, but still a rich life. Perhaps at times it was also a lonely life amidst the great responsibilities they often faced. On a couple of occasions during those prayer-times, I asked him whether he ever felt alone in the work of L'Abri. He gave me the same answer both times—that God had given him a wonderful wife with whom he could share the work, and that he was blessed by having children who were all Christians and actively interested in L'Abri. He was truly grateful for these things and did not take them for granted.

Communication and Truth

Dr. and Mrs. Schaeffer constantly stressed the importance of prayer as communication with God. L'Abri existed on the basis of prayer, as a demonstration of God's existence. In her book

L'Abri, Mrs. Schaeffer writes: "We prayed that God would bring the people of His choice, keep others away, send in the needed financial means to care for us all, and open His plan to us." Having prayed that God would bring to them the people of His choice, the Schaeffers loved them and cared for them. They reasoned that since communication with God through Jesus Christ is possible, so also true communication between human beings is possible.

It was a time when many writers, film-makers, and others were dealing with communication, and when many had concluded that real communication was *not* possible—whether in relation to God, among people, or even between man and woman in the marriage relationship. Although few Christians in the 1960s understood this, Dr. Schaeffer recognized the problem and sought to understand the work of the leading existential thinkers of the day—as seen, for example, in books like *No Exit* by Sartre and *The Foreigner* by Camus; or in films like *The Seventh Seal* and *The Virgin Spring* by Bergman, and *Blow-Up* by Antonioni. But for the Schaeffers communication was not just an abstract concept to be discussed in literature and film. It was something to be demonstrated as a reality in their own daily lives—in the abundant giving of their time.

I used to enjoy enormously the Saturday night discussions led by Dr. Schaeffer. I have many lovely memories of time spent by the fireplace in the living room of *Chalet les Mélèzes*, their home. Dr. Schaeffer always looked around the room very carefully, his eyes taking in who was there. Then he'd ask if anybody had any questions. Often a few moments of complete silence would follow. Not at all embarrassed, Schaeffer would say that he had never known a Saturday night without questions, and soon the questions came, one after the other, until very late at night. Dr. Schaeffer made the discussion relevant for those present, carefully taking into account what subjects they were studying, or what job they were doing, or what country they were from. Often when I was there, he referred to Dante, Petrarca, Michelangelo, and Leonardo, or to specific problems inherent to the Roman Catholic Church. Each one received a personal approach revealing a concern for which one felt touched and grateful. His answers were thorough, going to the roots of the problem.

At about 11 P.M. he usually stated that he wanted to stop soon because he still had his sermon to complete for tomorrow, but that he had time for one final question. By the time he had completed his answer, at least another hour would go by. The next morning during the service, I could pick up elements related to the previous evening; I could see that he had taken time to think further about them, and that he wanted to clarify certain points in light of the Bible.

I was eager to be there on Saturday nights. For several years I had been trying on my own to unfold the mysteries of life, and have savored other people's experiences and perceptions in what I had read. Dr. Schaeffer's way of thinking was stimulating, and I perceived the direction of his mind. I appreciated his curiosity and knowledge and his desire to relate it to the message of Christianity. Hearing the questions of people was also instructive, especially in light of their different backgrounds and countries. It was an unending parade! All the various nationalities, color of skin, ways of dressing—and with the hippie movement a variety of hair-styles, clothes, and colors.

Yet it was heartbreaking to see the consequences of the hippie lifestyle. Some were heavily addicted to drugs; some could not take care of themselves or their own children. There were couples, and girls on their own, expecting babies; there were girls with two or three children, each one by a different father. Young people who had been rejected—who had no place to go—found a home in L'Abri, where they were loved and cared for.

I saw the Schaeffers reaching out to them and giving them the message of hope through Christ. I saw Dr. Schaeffer sitting down on the floor or on the stairs talking to some who could not even stand up, being so heavily drugged. There were even those who were demon-possessed whom the Schaeffers were willing to have in their home and in contact with their children. They were willing to carry the burdens that all these multitude of people came with. Their life was busy indeed—meals to prepare, endless dishes to be washed, beds to be made, mountains of washing—and picking up the pieces of broken lives. Fortunately, many caring people became workers in L'Abri and shared the responsibilities for both the practical and spiritual needs. Often after a weekend in L'Abri I was so full of emotions that I wondered how the Schaeffers could persevere in their work. Each person brought his or her bundle of problems, and then the gospel stirred up their deepest feelings.

I saw many people being changed at L'Abri. Many became Christians; some did not. But I think that most went away with the knowledge that they had been loved—with a sense of worth and a clear idea of the existence of God, and with the reality of communication on both a divine and human level. Dr. Schaeffer was excited about those years in the 1960s. He enjoyed the discussions with the young people—their eager minds, their search for truth—though he hated the consequences of drugs and sin in the life of so many of them.

Out of his belief in the truth of the Bible, Dr. Schaeffer talked and preached with frankness, strength, and conviction. His message was indeed the Good News to lost people, but he never hid the difficulties one might face in becoming a Christian—difficulties from other people, even from our fellow Christians at times, and the temptations brought by Satan to deflect us from glorifying and loving God. Yet he emphasized continuously that the Christian can overcome Satan by the power of Christ at work in us. His message was not an optimistic one, but a real one based on the Bible and his own life experience.

Caring About My Country

Once or twice a year Hurvey Woodson would bring a number of Italian students up to L'Abri. For most people, coming to L'Abri was simply a question of whether or not to come, but for the Italians there were always numerous difficulties—family opposition, difficulties with passports, last-moment conflicts and indecision. It was a trial of patience and trust for Hurvey and Dorothy in Italy, while in L'Abri there was excited preparation for their arrival. Dr. Schaeffer used to say: "When fifteen Italians are coming, they always seem many more than fifteen of any other nationality." Those groups were indeed full of vitality!

Dr. Schaeffer arranged special lectures and discussion groups for these Italians, and I would translate. He touched a number of subjects dealing with various disciplines from literature, art, and philosophy (with which I was more familiar from my own studies), to science and theology (which I did not know). Although he could not speak Italian, he knew enough to realize when I was making a mistake. He would then repeat his sentence, and give me an opportunity to correct my translation. If his terminology was somewhat difficult to translate, since Italian is not as precise as English, he made my job as easy as possible by stating his ideas clearly and carefully. One concept always led to the next, respecting the step-by-step way the human mind works.

Occasionally Dr. Schaeffer was invited to go and speak in Italy, and I was then asked to go and translate for him. We would travel by train between Switzerland and Italy. Usually just he and I went, since Mrs. Schaeffer stayed behind to carry on the work of L'Abri in Huémoz. He spent the travel time preparing for his lectures, giving me an outline of what he was going to say so that I would have it in my mind.

He liked to analyze the Italian culture, touching on the problems inherent to the country itself and on the problems of the Christians and the non-Christians there. He was perceptive in his study of Italian culture and politics. His observations were well analyzed, and he brought the refreshing perspective of a Protestant Christian who had not been bound by Roman Catholic thinking either by faith or emotions.

After the conference, on the way back on the train, we would exchange impressions and opinions about all we had just lived through. At times he expressed his dismay about some of the missionaries in Italy—for their lack of understanding about the culture in which they were working, and for their lack of interest in trying to explore it through the arts and literature. He believed that it is important to spend time studying secular subjects, and that these need to be studied in light of the Bible. He saw that Italian evangelical Christians often did not perceive their own situation clearly either, and he prayed constantly for a revival there. I valued his opinions, and I was grateful for these exchanges. It especially meant a lot to me that Dr. Schaeffer cared enough about my country and my people to pray for them, to be

willing to undertake the discomfort of traveling, and the fatigue
of preparing the lectures when he already had so much to do in
Switzerland. When the Schaeffers saw a need, whether in a
person or in a country, they prayed about it first, but they also
took the action their prayers required. They realized there is a
time when the door is open and it does not last forever.

When I went to Dr. Schaeffer's funeral, some of these memories, along with many others, flooded into my mind. The flash-
backs were further nourished as I saw again the faces of the
Schaeffer family and of so many other dear friends. Their signs
of sorrow were a reflection of mine. Udo Middlemann, Dr.
Schaeffer's son-in-law, was at my side. He sensed my emotions
and drew closer. Looking intently into my eyes he asked,
"Where would you be if it were not for him?" While I was still
looking in his eyes and wondering where he too would be, he
asked in turn the same question about himself. "Where indeed,"
I thought, "would so many be?"

"Through Dr. Schaeffer's ministry to me, everything necessary for me to repent of my religious liberalism and become a Bible-believing Christian was demonstrated in life and thought. This meant some radical changes for me in my ministry, but the hopelessness, the meaninglessness, and the despair have never once returned to haunt me."

Louis Gifford Parkhurst

Louis Gifford Parkhurst, Jr., is Pastor of First Christian Church of Rochester, Minnesota. During the last few years of Dr. Schaeffer's life, Rev. Parkhurst was both a close friend and a pastor to the Schaeffer family when they were in Rochester. He is a past president of the Rochester Evangelical Pastors Fellowship. He received the M.Div. from Princeton Theological Seminary and the M.A. in philosophy from the University of Oklahoma. Rev. Parkhurst is the author of *Francis Schaeffer: The Man and His Message* (Tyndale) as well as the editor of a ten volume series of Charles Finney's works (Bethany). He lives with his wife and their two children in Rochester.

The room in Chalet les Mélèzes which served as the Schaeffer's bedroom and Dr. Schaeffer's study for seventeen years.

Chapter Eight

The Quiet Assurance of Truth

by

Louis Gifford Parkhurst, Jr.

Pastor and Friend

Dr. Schaeffer carefully and courteously stepped around those sitting on the stairs as he came down from his second-story bedroom to the crowd waiting below. The little green house on Fifteenth Avenue in Rochester, Minnesota, had become the center for "the Monday night discussions," even before L'Abri had officially moved its North American headquarters here in 1980. Dressed in his white coat and knickers, he took his chair near the hallway so those sitting in the downstairs bedroom, the L'Abri office, the kitchen, dining room, and living room could hear the conversation. With the quiet assurance of truth, he asked, "Well, let's begin the way we did last time. Are there any questions?"

This particular night a young man began to ask questions obnoxiously, and kept challenging Dr. Schaeffer with the words, "You Christians say . . . ." Some time later I found out more about the young man from a close friend of the Schaeffers who knew him. He had recently entered a Ph.D. program at Mayo Medical School and had come to the discussion with the express purpose of arguing with Dr. Schaeffer. Although he was abusive and continually made dogmatic statements against Christianity, Dr. Schaeffer neither lost his refined attitude nor allowed the man to walk over him. Each time he was cut off, Dr. Schaeffer would calmly reply, "Well, if you would just let me finish my sentence . . . ," only to be cut off again. Unable to blow Dr. Schaeffer's composure, the young man eventually backed off, but with a deep and lasting impression having been made upon him. Some time later the young man remarked that "Dr. Schaeffer was the first Christian I could not make angry, who would not lash out or be driven into a corner." And because he had not been beaten down in an "argument with Dr. Schaeffer," he went on to have a new appreciation for the Christian faith which he had intended to discredit, eventually discussing Christianity openly with others in his Ph.D. program.[1]

The End of Liberalism

Prior to 1979, I would have been an unlikely candidate to be praying with the Schaeffers that night as I listened to the discussion. I first heard of "Schaeffer" in the Spring of 1976, when my church custodian, a well-read and devout Bible-believing Christian, gave me two of Dr. Schaeffer's books, *No Little People* and *No Final Conflict*. I grudgingly finished reading *No Final Conflict*, and knew I didn't want to read any more of this man "Schaeffer." So I hid his books away in the bookcase, dismissing him as "just another conservative." By education and experience, I knew that conservatives were conservative because they were "dumb, ignorant, and stupid." If they would only read, study, and think through the issues, I felt surely they would come to think as I did. After all, I had advanced degrees in both philosophy and theology.

With my theological education, I knew that the Bible was full of mistakes, and as a pastor and preacher I was responsible for separating the wheat from the chaff in Scripture in order to feed others the "sifted and refined" Bread of Life. Bible study was spent deciding what Jesus had *really* said, then pointing out what biases the Gospel writers had, and how they had put their own ideas into Jesus' mouth as they tried to answer the current problems of their own churches. I knew how to "psychologically" explain away almost every miracle. And the mere mention of the real existence of Adam, Eve, or a personal Devil was embarrassing.

By 1978, however, when I was in my third church, I had

thought through my liberal indoctrination to its own logical conclusions of emptiness and despair, and of intellectual, moral, and spiritual bankruptcy. As Dr. Schaeffer himself would have said, "A rationalistic man had played the game to the end, and was in despair because he could not find any answers." I prayed, studied, and preached from the Bible, but inside I felt lost and hopeless because I did not have a Bible-believing base upon which to build my life and ministry. I could no longer tell truth from error in the Scriptures. I was enslaved to my emotions and continually being buffeted by overwhelming temptations. I had seen only a few "born again" under my ministry, and that was strictly by the providential grace of God in spite of me. As with most liberals, I believed that making Christians was little more than making church members.

After Dr. Schaeffer arrived in Rochester, he was interviewed by a reporter from the local newspaper, the *Post-Bulletin*. I read the article at a time when I had almost given up hope, and somehow found out where he was living. I went to the rented brown townhouse and announced, "I just have to talk with Dr. Schaeffer!" Immediately Susan Schaeffer Macaulay and Edith Schaeffer very cordially invited me in for tea with Dr. Schaeffer, and I began to ask him some of the questions that troubled me. I did not know that he had just been told by some of his doctors that he had perhaps only six weeks to six months to live. Though I had been invited in during what could have been the last precious days of his life, he made me feel that he cared about me personally, and he never indicated that he had just been given reason to be very concerned about his own physical health. At the time, I also did not realize that he was a highly respected Christian thinker. He was the very form of meekness and humility, reaching out to help a troubled soul that the Lord had sent him in answer to prayer.

Later, I learned that I was one of the very first in Rochester to come knocking at his door with questions, and that the first few who came had given him hope that God was giving him more time for ministry, and that he would have a new ministry here in Rochester. Rather than personal defeat or an unwanted displacement from his home in Switzerland, Dr. Schaeffer saw this as an opportunity for an extension of his mission field. His cancer thus became an occasion for a new outreach to the medical community—in the fight for the sanctity of life and issues of medical ethics, but equally for the salvation of the physicians and others whom God brought into his life.[2]

Answered Questions

I did not become a Bible-believing Christian after those few brief moments with Dr. Schaeffer. He invited me to attend some of his seminars with the hospital chaplains and the medical students to learn more. I will never forget a meeting with medical students in Methodist Hospital when I raised my hand and asked a question about predestination, and got a very brief answer. Later, in a visit with Mrs. Schaeffer, she told me how they prayed for all of their meetings, and then added, "We sometimes pray that no one will ask a question about *predestination* or some other *technical question* that should rightly concern Christians in the right places, because we are trying to do evangelism and don't want to get sidetracked arguing issues that will prevent the gospel from being heard by the non-Christians who are present." I have never told Mrs. Schaeffer, who had not been at this meeting, "That's just what I did!"

By early 1979, God graciously gave me all the answers I needed to have before I could be intellectually honest when I bowed before Him and accepted His Word as true. Everything came together for me during one of the episodes of *How Should We Then Live?* as it was being shown in the John Marshall High School Auditorium. I then became a Bible-believing Christian, once Dr. Schaeffer had answered my questions in these crucial areas:

1. He answered the philosophical and theological questions that were crucial before I could believe that the Bible was true in all that it affirms—in all matters, including historical, scientific, and ethical concerns.

2. He convinced me that Christianity was true to reality—that the teachings of the Bible really correspond to what is, to the nature and character of God, as well as to the world as created and sustained by God. If he had not been able to do this, then

any theological system of thought that I might have adopted would have simply "hung in the air." As a system it might be "good for me, or it might answer some questions, or might be helpful to others," but I would have no assurance that it would be ultimately true.

3. He demonstrated that the Bible and Christian truth are internally consistent as a whole system of thought which answers the questions reality challenges us to ask.[3]

4. He demonstrated that the Christian faith, with its teachings about life and morality, is the only practical guide to living in this world, and the only sure guide to the next.

5. He demonstrated that the Bible is supported by a great deal of archaeological evidence, and that no portion of the Bible has ever been disproven by serious scientific investigation.

6. He lived as though the supernatural were real. He prayed, and he knew and taught that God would answer prayer in the midst of the spiritual battles Christians fight.

7. He personally demonstrated the kind of love and life that a Bible-believing Christian should have for God and others. His caring, compassionate, and kind attitude commended his teaching. He managed to do what he said all Christians should do: "We have two callings: to show forth the existence of God and to show forth the character of God (His love and His holiness) at the same time. We can only do this in His strength and help." Though Dr. Schaeffer was the first to admit that he was not perfect, he did this in a very real way.[4]

Bowing Before God

Through Dr. Schaeffer's ministry to me, everything necessary for me to repent of my religious liberalism and become a Bible-believing Christian was demonstrated in life and thought. This meant some radical changes for me in my ministry, but the hopelessness, the meaninglessness, and the despair have never once returned to haunt me. I had to tell my church that I was now a Bible-believing Christian, and that I was going to be preaching differently. I told them what historic Biblical Christianity was, and how it differed from what many of us had learned. I told them that I would be standing against religious liberalism in every way that I possibly could, because I knew by experience and had seen in others how totally destructive liberalism is. I began to take some stands on social concerns that were radically different from the immorality of our day; and I began to preach about the evils of abortion. In all of these difficult times Dr. Schaeffer stood with me in prayer and in giving good advice.

When I got straightened out by the Lord, then the Lord was able to use me. For the first time, I saw several people both inside and outside of my church come to saving faith in Jesus Christ. I saw victims of incest leave the type of life their victimization had influenced them to adopt, and I saw them embrace God as their new and real Father who would never abuse them. I saw people come to the Lord from many varied walks of life. At the same time, God enabled me to have the writing ministry that I had longed for: I simply needed to have truth to be empowered to write.

Dr. Schaeffer helped me find a faith that was grounded in God, His Word, and the reality of the world in which I lived. He would often say, "There is only one reason to become a Christian, and that is because Christianity is true—the truth of total reality. Christian revelation answers the questions, and these answers are not self-generated, but are given by God in the Bible."

When he was asked why all good thinkers didn't come to believe, he said, "According to the Christian answer, we are not to be and cannot be autonomous in metaphysics and morals. But to become Christians, people have to give up being autonomous, and many people do not want to give up being autonomous. To become a Christian, you must bow, both metaphysically and morally, before the God who is there. In evangelism it is important to make people Christians and then help them live consistently as Christians."

A Reason to Live

The next few years sped by swiftly for Dr. Schaeffer as he wrote books, attended seminars and L'Abri conferences, and helped many different groups and individuals in between his treatments for cancer. The truth of God's existence gave him meaning for life and a reason to keep on fighting. He knew that he was involved in a spiritual battle; therefore, he had a reason to keep on keeping on. Speaking of his cancer and the other abnormalities of this life, he often stressed that "We live in a fallen world. The world is not now as God created it. There are lots of things in history that God didn't mean to be there. The revolt against God is real. There is meaning to the battle that we have in the heavenlies. On the basis of truth being there we are given our intensity for our work."

His intensity carried over into his room at St. Mary's Hospital during his last few months of life. Often when I would call on him, he would be working on his last book, *The Great Evangelical Disaster*. He even took the time to read and discuss the *Christianity Today* articles on the most recent meeting of the World Council of Churches when I rushed them over to him, and he managed to include these ideas in the book. Since my faith was destroyed by liberalism, I hope that everyone will take seriously the call Dr. Schaeffer made in that book, made literally with his dying breath.

When I think of the last few months of his life, I really am amazed. In December 1983, he was flown back from Switzerland at the edge of death. But during January and February, he regained enough strength to complete his work on *The Great Evangelical Disaster* in time to meet the publication deadline and to have it ready for his last college seminar tour. Some have criticized the fact that he spent the last few weeks of his life under the pressure of a demanding schedule speaking at ten Christian colleges across the country. Yet he would have it no other way, and undoubtedly it was the urgency of this last effort which sustained him in the closing months of his life. He saw the same trends of compromise and accommodation, which he had known from an earlier battle fifty years ago, on the rise within evangelical circles. In the face of this, he felt a responsibility and calling to do whatever he could to reverse the trend.

Balance

Francis Schaeffer was one of this century's great Christian leaders for a reason. A.W. Tozer once wrote, "The creative religious thinker is not a daydreamer, not an ivory tower intellectual carrying on his lofty cogitations remote from the rough world. He is more likely to be a troubled, burdened man weighed down by the woes of existence, occupied not with matters academic or theoretical, but the practical and the personal." Dr. Schaeffer met all of these criteria and was a clear example of the kind of person Tozer was describing. He was "completely honest and transparently sincere." He was "courageous." His thinking carried a "moral imperative." He was "ready to obey truth without reservation." He avoided the pitfall Tozer recognized: "I have met Christians with sharp minds but limited outlook who saw one truth and, being unable to relate it to other truths, became narrow extremists, devoutly cultivating their tiny plot, naively believing that their little fence enclosed the whole earth." And finally, Dr. Schaeffer was a man of worship and praise. Tozer wrote, "Man is a worshiper and only in the spirit of worship does he find release for all the powers of his amazing intellect."[5] Worship and praise so central for Dr. Schaeffer in keeping his priorities in balance that he said, *"True Spirituality* is the only one of my books that I read over and over again."

But, Dr. Schaeffer was also a sensitive human being who knew joys as well as sorrows. He could laugh and joke, and he had a special love for children. The last time my son Jonathan, who was seven at the time and who has Down's syndrome, was with Dr. Schaeffer, he picked him up and hugged him. In that very personal moment for the two of them, Jonathan reached up and pulled Dr. Schaeffer's white beard in a quick and totally unexpected action. Dr. Schaeffer spontaneously laughed a big laugh and threw his head back in a way that I will never forget. You could tell that he enjoyed that hug along with the unintimidated tug on his beard.

True Spirituality

To some, this portrait may seem unrealistically glowing. However, I knew Dr. Schaeffer during the darkest episodes of his life with respect to his diagnosis and treatments for terminal cancer. By the time he learned he had cancer, the Word of God and the Spirit of God had accomplished so much in the transformation of his personality, his heart and mind, that he truly had become as I and others have described him here. Whatever his faults in his younger years, he had learned the lessons of "true spirituality" in his later years.

Perhaps the key to understanding Dr. Schaeffer's life was his commitment to daily obedience in the power of Jesus Christ moment-by-moment. Even though he spoke a great deal about lack of perfection in this life, he knew that everyone, by the power of the indwelling Holy Spirit, could obey Christ moment-by-moment. When he failed in this, as we all do, he would bring his sin before God and ask for forgiveness and personal renewal. Indeed, perfection is not possible in this life, and to expect it in this life is not Biblical. But sanctification is the spiritual reality we are to pray for daily, as we exercise obedient faith in the power of the indwelling Spirit of Christ. This Dr. Schaeffer described as "true spirituality"; his life was a vibrant example of what it can mean.

He will be dearly missed by those who knew him and loved him. He helped so many of us personally. Yet, as important as we believe him to be, he would point us beyond himself to the Lord he loved and served, and who made his ministry effective. To honor his memory, we would do well to study the Scriptures diligently and prayerfully, learn the language of our culture, and then find new and better ways to do the work of Christ in our time and place—so many may find the Lamb as their Lord and Savior.

"What impressed me most. . .was that the Schaeffers believed in prayer, and that their prayers were answered often in a very direct way. . . . It was so different than prayer so often is—not just a blind hope, but in faith, believing that God did hear and that He would answer. . . . I knew God had answered."

Anky Rookmaaker

Anky Rookmaaker is the founder and current general sec-retary of Help a Child, Inc., an international organization to provide assistance to impoverished children in Africa, India and other Third-World countries. Her husband, Hans Rook-maaker, who died in 1977, was a distinguished art historian on the faculty of the Free University of Amsterdam. Mrs. Rookmaaker and her husband knew Francis and Edith Schaeffer well and worked with them for more than twenty-five years. The Rookmaakers were also the founders of the Dutch branch of L'Abri Fellowship, and Mrs. Rookmaaker is still active as a L'Abri member. She has three children and is living currently in the Netherlands.

Sunday morning service in the L'Abri chapel

Chapter Nine

Lifting up
Holy Hands

by
Anky Rookmaaker
Friend and Co-worker

It was 1948 in Amsterdam that we, my husband Hans and I, first met the Schaeffers. We were attending the Congress of the International Council of Christian Churches (ICCC). Francis Schaeffer was the European secretary of the Congress and was kept very busy handling the many arrangements as well as speaking. On Sunday we heard him preach, and I was so impressed with his message that I can still remember, now almost forty years later, that it was on John 17. Being a very recent Christian at that time, I often had difficulty understanding the sermons I heard in the small Dutch Reformed Church of which I had become a member. I knew I was a Christian, although a very immature one. Both Hans and I had come from non-Christian families. Hans became a Christian first, in a prisoner of war camp in Poland during World War II. When he came back to Holland after the war, he convinced me of the truth of the Bible, and I gave myself to Christ. But coming into the church with no Christian background, it was difficult for me to understand its language. By contrast Schaeffer's preaching was so clear and understandable that it left an unforgettable impression upon me.

Black American Music
I had promised to do some typing for the Congress, and one evening my husband (we were not yet married at the time,

though we were engaged) said that he would accompany me to the office. Hans had studied art history, but his hobby was collecting black American music. He had already started his collection when he was sixteen by saving up the ten cents pocket money he got each week to spend on secondhand phonograph records. At that time a used record cost about forty cents; so every four weeks he would add another to his collection. During the whole month he played the record continuously, and then exchanged it with a friend who had the same hobby. In this way Hans and his friend built up a large record collection and became experts in the black music of America.

Hans thought that an American could perhaps give him more information about black music. So he accompanied me to the office, thinking this would provide a good opportunity to meet some Americans and ask them some questions. When we arrived, Francis Schaeffer was there; Hans went over to him and asked him if they could spend some time talking together. Schaeffer looked at his watch and said he could only give Hans half an hour. And so they went away together for a short talk. When I saw Hans the next day, I asked him if he got his questions answered. He said no—because he never got around to asking them. Instead he said, they had had a fascinating talk until 4:00 A.M., mostly about modern art and its background.

A Common Path

At the time of this first meeting, of course, we did not realize how much this encounter would influence our lives. In the following years, whenever the Schaeffers visited Holland we always met with them. We talked especially about the "children for Christ" work which the Schaeffers had started in Europe, and they asked us to help with it in our own country. It was an outreach to children from the street who were invited into your home once a week to teach them from the Bible. The Schaeffers wrote the Bible lessons, which were published many years later in their book *Everybody Can Know* (Tyndale House). At that time this was quite a new method in Holland, and new especially for my own church. For many years I have done this with my own children, bringing their friends into our home. The way the

Schaeffers approached the Bible was important not only for the children, but for me personally as I also learned much from the studies.

During these visits to Holland, Francis and Hans often visited at museums together, afterwards talking through the night about the art they had seen, but also about many different things. It was remarkable to me how the Lord brought them together, and in such unexpected ways. Hans was studying art history at that time at the University of Amsterdam, and each year the University organized an excursion for the students to another country. (Some years later, after receiving his doctorate, Hans also did this for his students.) He would travel to Florence or London or to other places of special interest for art historians. Time and again Hans came home and asked, "Whom do you think I ran into?" in Florence, or London, or wherever he had been. It was always Francis Schaeffer. Sometimes they happened to meet without even knowing that the other would be there at the same time. Once they met unexpectedly on a street in London. In talking together, they discovered that their thinking had been developing in the same direction quite independently of each other since they hadn't met in months. Probably that was not so surprising when we remember that it was the same Holy Spirit that led them both. I know Hans was very grateful for these talks and for the oneness in Christ he so often experienced as they shared ideas and influenced each other.

I Do Not Know Where I Would Have Turned

What would our lives be without the Schaeffers? Most of these things happened before L'Abri started (in 1955). Already when the Schaeffer family lived in Champéry, Switzerland, beginning in 1949, we were in regular contact. And when the time came that the Schaeffers were to be put out of Switzerland in February of 1955, we heard this directly from them through carbon copies of Edith's letters to her own family. Of course, we were shocked, but gradually the shock changed to excitement as we heard all that the Lord did to start the L'Abri work in the Swiss village of Huémoz.

From the time of our first meeting till the beginning of L'Abri

I had a very difficult time in our own church. Coming from outside the church, it was difficult to understand all its rules and traditions. I attended church regularly, twice each Sunday, but it did not mean very much to me and I felt disappointed. I am sure that this was not only the fault of the church, but also my own. I neglected my daily Bible reading, and my spiritual life became very poor. I did not know if I could continue as a Christian. Often it seemed to me that people from outside the church, for example my own parents, were more human than the people inside the church. Of course, that was not true, but I felt like it was. Reformed people in Holland seldom talk about their faith and their love of God, so it is often difficult to see a real love of God existing in their lives. I am sure that it was as much my own fault as theirs; but I became so indifferent to all spiritual things. After long discussions with my husband, we decided in the end that we needed the Schaeffers' help.

L'Abri had just started, and we took the step to go to Switzerland with our three small children. I will never forget the first time we were there in Huémoz. There were very few guests, but we with our small children must have given everyone a lot of trouble, though they never complained to us. The children, of course, did not know any English, and they felt very unhappy with all the people around them whom they could not understand. Mrs. Schaeffer did her best to give them nice meals. She made ice cream, lovely cakes with icing. She tried hard to please them and get them to eat, but the only thing they wanted was dry bread and milk. Hans and I enjoyed our meals, especially since it was during mealtimes that we had long discussions. At that time everyone who came was a personal guest in the Schaeffers' home. (The Farel House study program and the addition of other chalets came some years later.) Meals especially were a time to ask your questions and get them answered. Often the meals and discussions around the table went on till late into the night. If we had not gone to L'Abri I don't know where I would have turned. Our stay there "saved" my life.

Believing in Prayer

What impressed me most during that first visit to L'Abri in Switzerland was that the Schaeffers *believed* in prayer, and that their prayers were answered often in a very direct way. I remember one evening at dinner when we prayed for a student from behind the Iron Curtain who was studying in Switzerland and was staying for a weekend at L'Abri. He had repeatedly failed his exams in Switzerland, because he did not know enough of the language. His future hung in the balance, and he was desperate to pass. Although he had worked hard, he had given up all hope of passing. I remember very clearly praying for the young student at dinner that night. It was different than prayer so often is—not just a blind hope, but in faith, believing that God did hear and that He would answer. During the time we were still in Switzerland, he tried the exams a final time and passed. I knew God had answered.

This is just one example, but it was by no means the only time prayers were clearly answered. The Schaeffers had such a different attitude about prayer than the Christians I knew in Holland. They prayed for specific things and they expected an answer, even if it was not always the answer they had hoped for. I had never encountered that attitude before. Dr. Schaeffer helped me further understand prayer by preaching one Sunday on the verse, "I will therefore that men pray everywhere lifting up *holy hands,* without wrath or doubting" (1 Timothy 2:8, KJV, emphasis added). In his sermon he went through the whole Bible explaining that "holy hands" were very important for our prayer life. If we sin knowingly and we do not regret and confess this sin, the Lord won't hear our prayers. And if there is sin between us and God, then our hands are not "holy." This came as a revelation to me. Later on I had many more talks with both Francis and Edith about prayer, and I will be forever grateful to them that they gave of their time to teach me.

That first visit to Switzerland helped me through a difficult time in my spiritual life, and it also changed my attitude toward the church in Holland, of which I am still a member. It seemed as if after I came back home, I listened in a different way. Now in my own church I heard the same truths of the Bible that Dr. Schaeffer had explained to me, and I am grateful for its faithful Bible teaching.

Another verse which has been important to me is: "The Lord is near. Be anxious for nothing, but in everything by prayer and supplication with thanksgiving let your requests be made known to God" (Philippians 4:5, 6, NASB). In my family, in my part in the L'Abri work in Holland, and in my starting the work of "Help a Child" for poor children in underdeveloped countries, this verse has given me strength and assurance over the years.

The Mark of a Christian

Of course, it was not only the meaning of prayer which I came to understand at L'Abri. There is so much more, but I will mention only one other thing here. I have always found fighting and criticism among Christians hard to accept, because it does so much harm to God's kingdom. It is difficult to understand why this exists among Christians. The mark of the Christian should be that they love one another (John 13:35). But so often the mark is missed. It is not easy to overlook criticism, especially if it is directed at someone you love who is being wrongly criticized. This happened to my husband, it happened to Dr. Schaeffer, and it happens to every Christian to some extent. But in response to unjust criticism Schaeffer often said, "Don't fight back, but wait on the Lord to fight for you." As the Bible says in many places: "Do not say, 'I will repay evil'; wait for the Lord, and He will save you" (Proverbs 20:22, NASB). Or, "Never take your own revenge, beloved, but leave room for the wrath of God, for it is written, 'Vengeance is Mine, I will repay, says the Lord'" (Romans 12:19, NASB). Or as Jeremiah wrote, "Let me see Thy vengeance on [my enemies[; For to Thee I have set forth my cause" (Jer. 20:12). And many more could be cited. Schaeffer helped me see that if we are convinced that we have done the right thing, then we can simply leave it with the Lord in prayer and wait for Him, because He will judge in a righteous way. I had found this a difficult lesson to learn because, in ourselves, we would rather fight back when we are attacked. If we as individuals, and if our churches and organizations, would practice this Biblical truth I am sure we would have fewer difficulties.

I have been greatly privileged to have had so much contact with both Francis and Edith Schaeffer. Hans and I were the first workers for L'Abri in Holland, and it was always a joy when they came to our country. Many people think of L'Abri as a Christian work for intellectuals; and it is true that many intellectuals found answers to their questions and Christ as the Savior at L'Abri. But I am not an intellectual, and I never felt out of place at L'Abri, even after my husband Hans died almost ten years ago. On the contrary—first as a L'Abri worker, then as a member, and now in my work with Help a Child—I have always felt accepted and loved, not only by Francis and Edith Schaeffer, but also by the younger generation of L'Abri workers and members. I love my church in Holland, but I feel home at L'Abri.

The last time I saw Dr. Schaeffer was the summer before he died—in Knoxville, Tennessee, the last L'Abri conference with him as the main speaker. He was too ill to greet us all personally, but he waved and he smiled. A world without Francis Schaeffer can never be the same world again. But I am grateful for the times that we were together, for his friendship and for his love and care. Through Hans, my husband, I became a Christian, but through Francis and Edith Schaeffer I remained one. I thank the Lord for them.

"Few people realize the personal sacrifice Dr. Schaeffer made, especially in the last few weeks of his life. ... It was his love for the church and its need to hear his final message that Francis Schaeffer could not stop. During those last few weeks, he was literally kept alive by the prayers of God's people and his strong desire to see the church purified and strengthened."

Melinda Delahoyde

Melinda Delahoyde is the former Director of Education for Americans United for Life, and is currently active in the prolife movement, as a writer, speaker, and board member for the Christian Action Council. She received a B.A. in philosophy from the University of California and an M.A. in philosophy of religion from Trinity Evangelical Divinity School. She is the author of *Fighting for Life* (Servant) and co-editor of *Infanticide and the Handicapped Newborn* (Servant). Mrs. Delahoyde is a homemaker with two young children and lives with her husband in Raleigh, North Carolina.

*March to 10 Downing Street (the Prime Minister's Office),
London*

Chapter Ten

We Thought We Could Have It All

by
Melinda Delahoyde
Human Life Issues

Can one person really make a difference? Certainly in the issues of human life the battle can be overwhelming. Since 1973 over eighteen million unborn children have been killed in the wombs of their mothers. Even after birth, no baby which falls short of someone's idea of "quality" is safe, as handicapped babies that once would have lived are now being routinely starved to death. And as this mentality sinks deeper into the fabric of our society, it is not surprising that one of our governors would proclaim that the aged have a duty to go off and die.

Turning Point

Something went wrong somewhere on the road to the American dream. We know that the 1973 Supreme Court decision to legalize the killing of the unborn was the turning point. But it is important to remember how this happened. During the 1960s and early 1970s a relatively small number of abortion advocates aggressively pushed their agenda to legalize abortion. They realized the courts were the key to realizing their goal. But in the *Roe v. Wade* decision the Supreme Court gave them more than they could ever have hoped for. In one day the High Court wiped out every state law and local ordinance prohibiting abortion. Abortion became legal during all nine months of pregnancy and the unborn child was left helpless, without any legal protection.

To put it mildly, evangelical Christians were caught off guard. They were totally unprepared and ill-equipped to deal with the crisis. For most it was an issue which did not touch their lives personally. It was the stuff of newspaper stories, statistics, and television newscasts. Or it was just another example of the decline of morality in America. And if most evangelicals lacked any clear understanding of how and why abortion came to be legalized, they also lacked any idea of how to respond. On the whole, evangelical churches avoided doing anything on the grounds that it was "too political" or "too controversial." With evangelicals nowhere to be found in the fight, we can be thankful for Catholic friends who spoke out and organized on behalf of life.

In recent years, however, the picture is dramatically different. Proabortionists had predicted that resistance to abortion would rapidly disappear after the Supreme Court decision. Instead the prolife movement is flourishing, and it can no longer be dismissed as a "Catholic issue." Thirteen years after *Roe v. Wade*, it had become a broad-based movement drawing from every sector of American life. Remarkably, the voices of evangelicals are now often heard at the head of the battle for life, and Bible-believing Protestants have stepped to the forefront.

How did this change come about? Probably the greatest single reason for this change can be attributed to the life and work of Francis Schaeffer. It was he, along with friends such as Surgeon-General C. Everett Koop, who laid the groundwork for an evangelical response to abortion. It was Dr. Schaeffer's work, in theory and in practice, which gave a generation of Bible-believing Christians the courage and reason to stand for life.

Ideas Have Consequences

Dr. Schaeffer recognized that the 1973 *Roe v. Wade* decision was the turning point in the abortion issue. But he also realized that abortion is really the deadly expression of a much more basic problem. Abortion is not an isolated occurrence; it is the deadly fruit of a materialistic world view that places man at the center of the universe, and at the same time reduces him to a piece of "disposable junk." Abortion became possible because of a fundamental shift in the understanding of what human life is. In the Judeo-Christian view, man has infinite worth because he is created in the image of God. In the contemporary materialistic view, man is simply a link in the evolutionary chain—a complex combination of atoms and energy which came into existence by chance—with no intrinsic meaning, purpose, or worth. Dr. Schaeffer explained:

> The dilemma of modern man is simple: he does not know why man has any meaning. He is lost. Man remains a zero. . . . But if we begin with [God as the Personal Creator] and this is the origin of all else, then the personal does have meaning, and man and his aspirations are not meaningless.[1]

What Dr. Schaeffer saw so clearly was that the Judeo-Christian view and the materialistic view lead to totally opposite consequences. In the Judeo-Christian view, human life has eternal significance because each life is the personal creation of a loving, compassionate Creator. Every life therefore has value and dignity—whether a tiny helpless unborn baby, a handicapped child, or a man or woman approaching the end of life. But in the materialistic view of the secular world there is no God and no absolute moral order. "If man is . . . nothing more than the energy particle extended," Schaeffer wrote, ". . . he has no intrinsic worth. Our own generation can thus disregard human life. On the one end we will kill the embryo . . . and on the other end we will introduce euthanasia for the old."[2]

As Dr. Schaeffer often observed: "Abortion leads to infanticide leads to euthanasia." If we accept the principle that it is okay to kill babies before they are born, then why not after they are born—especially if we think they are imperfect or burdensome? And if we accept this further extension of the principle, certainly there is no compelling reason to keep alive the elderly person who is no longer able to care for himself. Abortion leads to infanticide leads to euthanasia—and there is no place to draw the line. As Dr. Schaeffer saw so clearly,

> Without the Judeo-Christian base which gives every
> individual an intrinsic dignity as made in the image of
> the personal-infinite Creator, each successive horror
> fails naturally into place. . . .[3]

For those of us who work almost daily with the human life issues, Dr. Schaeffer's analysis of these issues has been our stronghold. No one is "proabortion," as the prochoice people often emphasize. Instead, they say, the issue is always clouded. Abortion is right sometimes and wrong sometimes. It all depends on a woman's personal choice. Everything is relative and everything is okay, depending on your value system. Planned Parenthood tells us they are not proabortion. They are simply working for the freedom to choose (to kill your child).

The fundamental truths about abortion are deliberately clouded over and made hazy. How often in the midst of writing or speaking out against a proabortion opponent I have turned to Dr. Schaeffer's clear analysis of ideas and their consequences. Everything is not okay. Abortion is not simply a "social problem." Killing in the name of compassion is never right. The truly Biblical position of the sanctity of every human life is the only world view that provides an adequate basis for real love and compassion. Ideas have consequences, no matter who tells us they do not. American society has provided ample verification for the truth of Dr. Schaeffer's position. It is confirmed in the deaths of eighteen million unborn babies. It is confirmed by the routine starvation of "Baby Does" whose parents and doctors do not think they have lives worth living. It is confirmed in the withdrawal of care for the aged, and in a governor's statement that the elderly have a *duty* to die.

Lord of All Life

Abortion is not some "ivory tower" issue. Now is not the time for a nice discussion about the agonizing and complex aspects of abortion. Knowledge means action. That was the essence of Dr. Schaeffer's message. For many evangelicals it was a message they were not accustomed to hearing. They expected to hear someone speak on evangelism, salvation, or the "spiritual issues of the Christian life." No one of Dr. Schaeffer's stature or reputation had spoken out on an issue like abortion. It was controversial, political, and "worldly." Many Christians could hardly utter the *word* abortion, let alone converse about it in a public forum. Most thought it was something they would never have to think about. It was enough to attend church services and weekly Bible studies. But now one of the most prominent leaders in evangelicalism was saying it was not enough. To be a Christian meant that Christ was Lord in all of life. Innocent human life was being destroyed, and Christians above all have a duty to be involved. Schaeffer's entrance into one of the deepest moral and political crises of our time forced many evangelicals to confront the fact they could no longer live with a false division of "spiritual" and "worldly" concerns. Political involvement, ministering to women with crisis pregnancies, or setting up hospice care in your local community were spiritual works in God's eyes—just as much a Christian ministry as feeding the poor and hungry.

A great part of the Francis Schaeffer legacy can be seen in the thousands of Christians across the country who took Dr. Schaeffer seriously when he called for the Lordship of Christ in every area of their lives. Over the past several years God has given me the privilege of traveling across the country to work with Christians involved in prolife ministries. Again and again I hear the same story of how they became aware of the human life issues at a seminar given by Dr. Schaeffer. For some it was viewing *Whatever Happened to the Human Race?* that made them realize they could not stand quietly by on the abortion issue. Today these people have organized crisis pregnancy centers in their communities or have worked at the state level to enact laws that protect human life. Often these believers come to the task with few resources. But they are sincere followers of Christ who have taken God at His Word. They trusted that he would provide financial and spiritual resources to help women in their community. Many literally prayed their crisis pregnancy centers into existence. They have seen miracles as God opened up buildings, provided thousands of dollars, and gave them the opportunity to counsel young women in the most serious situations. For so many the courage to take that first step came from the example of Dr. Schaeffer. It is astounding to me to see the way in which God's Spirit quietly worked in the hearts of His people as Dr. Schaeffer spoke on the need for Christians' involvement in the human life issues. Seeds that were planted years ago have come to fruition so that today we witness thousands of Bible-believing Christians who are putting their faith to work.

Recently I heard a prolife leader make a contrast between the proabortion movement and the prochoice movement. He correctly observed that the proabortion machine was an elitist group of well-financed individuals who worked their will *over* the American public and not through them. Through the court system, the national media, and various government agencies, they pressed for their proabortion agenda in society. The prolife movement, in contrast, was a grass-roots phenomenon. With little money, and no support from the media or the courts, they have launched an offensive against abortion. They have spoken in churches and community groups. They have organized their towns and states to fight abortion. Although the prolife movement began as a small band of (mainly Catholic) activists, it has grown into a major social and political force in American life, with leadership coming increasingly from conservative evangelicals. Although Dr. Schaeffer was not the only Protestant to speak out on the issues, his public example and his words of exhortation to become involved were greatly used by God to encourage His people to fight the destruction of innocent human life.

The Practice of Truth

Francis and Edith Schaeffer had always exemplified balance in the Christian life. Truth demanded confrontation, but always loving confrontation. L'Abri was dedicated to the pursuit of Christian truth and the power of ideas. But the most intellectual studies were always carried out in the context of loving and sharing in a small family setting. Their approach to the prolife issues was not different. Being prolife meant more than being antiabortion. It meant sharing your resources with an unwed pregnant teenager, or ministering to a family whose first child had been born with a severe handicap. Picketing, lobbying, speaking out were all important, but not without the accompanying practical demonstration of the love of Jesus Christ.

This was a very strong message in *Whatever Happened to the Human Race?* and in the Schaeffers' lives. As a pastor, he had spent several hours each week helping a special child in his congregation whose parents could not afford expensive therapy sessions. The family had brought Dr. Schaeffer's mother to live with them during the last years of her life. Her care routine demanded extra time, energy, and love from every family member. Many unwed pregnant women had found care and compassion at L'Abri.

Dr. Schaeffer's exhortation to meet practical needs was exactly the balanced message evangelicals needed to hear. Not many who read or heard Dr. Schaeffer could walk away from their responsibility to minister to women and families in need. For years proabortionists had accused prolifers of being uncaring; often we heard the words, "You care about the child, but what about the pregnant woman?" From the very beginning Dr. Schaeffer's life and his words said that he did care. His was exactly the approach evangelicals needed to take on abortion if they were to be faithful to Christ.

Today hundreds of crisis pregnancy centers have sprung up around the nations. Many of them are sponsored by evangelical churches and staffed with volunteers from local congregations. One article referred to these centers as "a movement of the Holy Spirit that is sweeping the country." Christians are making a difference and showing that abortion is not the answer for anyone—not for the unborn child and not for its mother. Very seldom now do I hear the argument that we just do not care.

In our own family the practice of truth has taken on a special meaning. For years my husband, Bill, and I have been involved in the prolife movement. If I had to pick my area of expertise in the human life issues, it would be infanticide and the nontreatment of handicapped newborn babies. In January of 1983, several years after I had begun speaking on this issue, our first child, Will, was born. Will has Down's syndrome. Suddenly

Bill and I found ourselves thrown into a new world of special children and their families. Over the past years I have had opportunities to minister to and with these families. God has shown me how important it is for Christians to meet those practical needs a family with a special child can have. It may be just going to the grocery store or baby-sitting once a week. But whatever we do, it can make the difference between a healthy, growing family situation and a shattered family unit. It takes time and sacrifice for us to be there to listen to a mother share her grief about her baby and her lost expectations for a "perfect child." It takes extra energy for us to learn the care routine for a severely handicapped child so that a mother can have a day off. But every effort we make has lifelong benefits for the child and the family. We must be more than anti-infanticide or anti-euthanasia. We must bring the love and compassion of Jesus to some very tough situations.

Counting the Cost

Within the evangelical community, fighting abortion, infanticide, and euthanasia were not met with the support and enthusiasm one might expect. Many evangelicals simply refused to get involved. Churches that would have welcomed a seminar on the basics of spiritual growth closed their doors to a film series on abortion. That Dr. Schaeffer should risk his reputation, friendships, and associations to fight in such a controversial issue was a sign of the importance of abortion and the life issues. It was also a sign of how much true obedience to Christ could cost in American society.

Although it would never have occurred to Dr. Schaeffer, many would have understood if he had refused to take up the gauntlet on abortion. He had fought for Christian truth his entire life. L'Abri, and his books, tapes, and film series, had already taken much personal sacrifice. His health was failing. Undertaking such a work could only hurt him physically. It would have been so easy to pass the work to someone else. Instead he chose to speak out for truth. Few people realize the personal sacrifice

Dr. Schaeffer made, especially in the very last few weeks of his life.

I met Dr. Schaeffer in November of 1983 in Chicago. At that time plans were underway for the publication of the book *The Great Evangelical Disaster*. He and Mrs. Schaeffer were finishing up a speaking tour in the United States. At that meeting Dr. Schaeffer impressed upon all of us the importance of the message in *The Great Evangelical Disaster*. His love and concern for his fellow Christians, and the uncompromising stand the church must take on issues like abortion and infanticide, were foremost in his mind. Although his recent schedule had been hectic, he seemed in good health. Soon after our visit he returned to Switzerland. Only a few weeks later Dr. Schaeffer was taken gravely ill and was rushed to the United States. It should have signaled the end of all work. For weeks he could not read or write. It was only with the help of Lane Dennis that *The Great Evangelical Disaster* became a reality.

It was because of his love for the church and its need to hear his final message that Francis Schaeffer could not stop. In March 1984, he, Mrs. Schaeffer, and Franky Schaeffer began an exhausting ten-city speaking tour to launch his book and the film by the same name. For a person in excellent health their kind of schedule would have been grueling. But for a man dying of cancer it was unthinkable.

When I met Dr. Schaeffer again it was in March at the beginning of the tour. As he openly acknowledged, he was dying. Although his spiritual and intellectual vigor never waned, his physical strength had rapidly deteriorated. He left his bed in a succession of hotel rooms only for speaking engagements on the tour. Halfway through the tour he would undergo intense chemotherapy. Yet if his body was weak, his spirit was vibrant. With great clarity and passion, he spoke of the need for the church to stand strong in a secular age and of his deepening love for the Holy Scriptures. During those last few weeks, he was literally kept alive by the prayers of God's people and his strong desire to see the church purified and strengthened. Dr. Schaeffer completed the tour and returned to his home in Minnesota.

During the next six weeks, his health deteriorated rapidly until he died quietly at his home.

Radicals for Christ

Dr. Schaeffer's life had a subtle and deeper impact on the younger generation of Christians. For the "baby boom" evangelicals, the resistance, apathy, and personal sacrifice that Dr. Schaeffer endured for the prolife cause was a sign of what the future may hold for those who follow Jesus.

Many of us grew up believing that Christianity and the pursuit of the American Dream were compatible. After all, America was basically Christian. In our parents' day the media, the schools, and American culture in general reflected a consensus on basic Judeo-Christian values. We assumed that the same would be true for us; we thought we could "have it all" and that our culture would be sympathetic to the religious beliefs we cherished.

The U.S. Supreme Court decisions on abortion shattered these assumptions. As a nation we had decided that killing unborn, innocent babies was legal. For the first time since the slavery decisions certain members of the human race were excluded from membership in the human family. Abortion, as horrible as it was, was just the beginning. A fundamental change in American values had taken place. Because of that change, abortion became a watershed issued for many young evangelicals.

To be obedient to Christ meant that one had to speak out against this injustice—and speaking out was costly. Doctors who spoke against abortion and infanticide did so at the risk of losing patients or their jobs. From the beginning, the medical establishment, such as the AMA, had taken a firm proabortion stance. Nurses who had the courage to feed handicapped newborn children designated for starvation were sometimes terminated from their jobs. Journalists who sought the truth cases involving handicapped babies did so at their own risk. A graduate student at a prestigious American university was denied his Ph.D. when he had the courage to tell the world about

China's inhuman population control policy of forced abortion and infanticide.

For many of us, the response to abortion from sections of the American public showed us that we had entered a new kind of relationship with our society—that life in the future would not be so easy; that truly we are "aliens and strangers in the world" (1 Pet. 2:11, NIV).

Again, it is Dr. Schaeffer's lifetime example that has brought encouragement. When I met Dr. Schaeffer during the last years of his life, he told me that one of his fervent prayers had been that God would raise up a generation of radical, young believers who would challenge the secular juggernaut in American society. God is answering this prayer today. Around the country God is calling young Christian professionals to give up the "American Dream" and devote their talents and energies to work in the prolife movement or some other issue-oriented ministry. In every way these are the young leaders of society. During my years of full-time work in the prolife movement, I saw young law students from the nation's top law schools come for a summer of legal internship. They were underpaid and overworked, but they had given up the high salaries and glamour of the legal profession to serve Christ with their talents. Today some of these same young people have taken positions working to change laws and protect Christian civil liberties in our country. The story can be told many times over. In our own circle of friends we have seen accountants, doctors, and nurses who gave up well-paid careers because they felt God's call to minister full-time in these issues. For many, their commitment is a result of that same commitment they saw in the life of Francis Schaeffer. God continues to call Christians into the professions. But at the same time he is calling Christians out of our materialistic culture and raising up a generation of "radicals for Christ" to work in society.

The life and work of Dr. Francis Schaeffer are an example to us all. Again, I would ask the question, can one life make a difference? Perhaps Edith Schaeffer provided the best answer in her book *L'Abri*. In speaking about the success of the study center, she said that to the degree that she and Dr. Schaeffer and so many others had put self aside and sought obedience, God had blessed the work. So it was also in the life of Francis Schaeffer. To the degree that he obeyed, God blessed. The cost of obedience was great, and so too was the blessing. Are we willing to pay the cost to make a difference?

"Francis Schaeffer's impact on the practice of law by Christians surely equals that of many legal scholars. By standing firm on the truth of the Scriptures, and by taking a clear and costly stand on the crucial issues of the day, Schaeffer has deeply influenced the direction of law in this country."

John W. Whitehead

John W. Whitehead is founder and president of the Rutherford Institute, a national legal and educational organization that initiates and participates in numerous lawsuits in defense of free speech and free exercise of religion. The Institute also regularly publishes books and papers, and conducts seminars throughout the country on the priority issues of the day. A leading constitutional attorney, he has written ten books, including a trilogy, concerning the rise and effects of secularism, entitled *The Second American Revolution* (Crossway), *The Stealing of America* (Crossway), and *The End of Man* (Crossway). Whitehead lives with his wife and five children in Virginia.

Addressing prolife rally, Hyde Park, London

Chapter Eleven

By Teaching, By Life, and By Action

by
John W. Whitehead
Law and Government

Although I became a Christian in the fall of 1974, it was not until some eight months later that I began reading Francis Schaeffer. I was attending a small seminary in Los Angeles, and Schaeffer's books were required reading. Having just completed law school, I was searching for a way to make some practical sense out of my Christian experience and how it related to the rest of life. Until I read Schaeffer, Christianity had seemed to be merely a pietistic experience without any real relationship to social action or culture. Francis Schaeffer's book *The God Who Is There* immediately challenged me with the fact that Christianity does apply to the "real world." Schaeffer insisted that past generations of Christians had gravely erred by making a division between "faith" and the rest of life—that is, by placing the primary emphasis on "upper-story" religious experience, while relegating social, cultural, and legal concerns to a lower—and therefore inferior—level. In contrast to this, Schaeffer stressed that *all* of life is spiritual and integrated.

Throughout his work, Schaeffer emphasized the bond between a person's inner world view and his outward behavior. *A person's view* of man's nature and meaning, and of man's significance to the world around him, has direct bearing on *how he acts* in relation to others. Thus Schaeffer chronicled a progres-

179

sion of ancient and modern men of influence, indicating how
their core philosophies of life significantly affected the course of
art, literature, law, and social action. Although he had significant insights into philosophy and history, Schaeffer never considered himself a technical scholar or professional philosopher,
even though many others ascribed both titles to him. He considered himself foremost an *evangelist*, called to help others see the
truth of Christianity and acknowledge Jesus Christ as their Savior and Lord.

Being an evangelist, however, encompassed far more than
what most Christians would consider "evangelistic activity"—
witnessing, church visitation, Bible studies, prayer groups—
although all of these are certainly important. To Schaeffer, evangelism also meant showing the world that Christ is Lord not only
of "religious things," but of *all* things. Every Christian is called
by Christ to be the salt of the earth; and every Christian has the
responsibility to impact the world around him with the absolutes
found in the Bible. What the Bible teaches—concerning the
sacredness and uniqueness of human life, and man's relationship
to his fellowman—is God's own Word to us, and it is to be
consciously *acted out* across the whole spectrum of human life.

As a young Christian, one of the most important things I
learned from Schaeffer was the need, indeed the *obligation*, to
live out my faith in the world around me. This awareness naturally had an immediate impact upon my view of law and how I
would use my legal education. Thus I realized that my education
was to be used in the service of God, to effectuate *His* will, to
reflect *His* Lordship. But my struggle at that time was how to do
that.

The Foundation of Law

Schaeffer's emphasis on the integration of faith and the real
world forced me into an in-depth study of the roots and foundation of law. Through that study I realized that law, as it had been
taught to me in law school and through various books and texts,
had become distorted, especially in its historical sense. America's Constitutional foundations, for example, were established
by men who, although many were not Christians, generally

acknowledged the existence and supreme authority of a Creator and the absoluteness of certain bestowed rights. This foundational philosophy, however, has been increasingly eroded in *practice*. Thus laws, and the interpretation of those laws, are based more and more on man's arbitrary judgments rather than upon any concept of supreme authority or the absoluteness of certain rights.

As Schaeffer had pointed out in his works, a system that is based on man's perceived autonomy and man's arbitrary standards cannot tolerate those with true absolutes by which to judge all arbitrary standards. Throughout history, Biblical Christians have therefore been maligned by those who refuse to accept the authority of God and His laws. As America moves farther away from God's authority and laws, we can only expect these kinds of attacks to increase. Thus, it was not surprising that shortly after my study of the roots of law I was contacted by Christians who had encountered problems expressing their faith in the public schools.

That was 1976—a very important year for me and others who have become involved in law and government. That was the year that Francis Schaeffer published his book *How Should We Then Live?* This book, released with a ten-part film series, was, in my opinion, the first significant attempt by a Christian leader in our day to impart a Christian concept of history and develop a Christian world view. But the book had special significance for the area of law where Schaeffer discussed his concept of sociological law and its humanistic distortion. Specifically, his critique of Justice Oliver Wendell Holmes, Jr. and the Supreme Court was an important catalyst for me and other Christian lawyers interested in seeing society positively influenced by Christianity.

As Schaeffer noted, Holmes contended that law was based on the arbitrary wishes of society. "Truth is the majority vote of that nation that could lick all others," Schaeffer explained. "So when it comes to the development of a *corpus juris* the ultimate question is what do the dominant forces of the community want and do they want it hard enough to disregard whatever inhibition may stand in the way." Thus former Chief Justice of the United

States, Frederick Moore Vinson, claimed, "Nothing is more certain in modern society than the principle that there are no absolutes."[1]

Key Ideas

This contrast which Schaeffer made—between the relativistic modern view as opposed to the traditional affirmation that all man-made laws must be grounded in "the laws of Nature and Nature's God"—encouraged me to research further the historical background of modern law. Although some have criticized *How Should We Then Live?* on the grounds that it was not a scholarly work, it contained the seeds from which a generation of books has sprouted, including several of my own. But it was also a direct influence in the Christian activism of myself and many others.

In particular, Schaeffer introduced me to the work of Samuel Rutherford, especially his book *Lex Rex*. Rutherford, a seventeenth-century Scottish minister argued that the Bible, not man, is the final authority for law—a concept which did not sit well with European royalty at that time and cost Rutherford much harassment from state authorities. It was my subsequent study of Rutherford that led to many of my thoughts on law, and how to use and influence law in terms of Christian absolutes. Eventually this led me to found the Rutherford Institute, a civil liberties organization dedicated to defending those who are the victims of the distorted standards of our relativistic society.

Another key idea introduced in *How Should We Then Live?* was the premise that abortion is wrong, in light of the Bible's teaching on the sanctity of life and the dignity of each individual as created in the image of God. To my knowledge, Schaeffer was the first Protestant leader of major influence to begin to fight abortion on a large scale. As first outlined in *How Should We Then Live?*, Schaeffer's criticism of the *Roe v. Wade* decision, the 1973 Supreme Court ruling which legalized abortion on demand, was pivotal in accelerating Christian involvement in fighting abortion.

Schaeffer's critique of the abortion issue was the initial impetus for my own defense of the sanctity of human life. He illustrated clearly how the United States Supreme Court has become a ruling oligarchy. Schaeffer wrote, for example, "The [*Roe v. Wade*] ruling set up an arbitrary absolute by disregarding the intent of the Thirteenth and Fourteenth Amendments of the Constitution."[2] Especially important, he showed that our society is moving into an era where *men* are the law and where no absolutes govern the people who run our society. Schaeffer argued that unless this trend is impeded and reversed, we will find ourselves under an unrestrained authoritarian rule. Thus Schaeffer wrote:

> Law has only a variable content. Much modern law is not even based on precedent; that is, it does not necessarily hold fast to a continuity with the legal decisions of the past. Thus, within a wide range, the Constitution of the United States can be made to say what the courts of the present want it to say—based on a court's decision as to what the court feels is sociologically helpful at the moment. At times this brings forth happy results, at least temporarily; but once the door is opened, anything can become law and the arbitrary judgments of men are king.[3]

Schaeffer warned further:

> The Supreme Court has the final voice in regard to both administrative and legislative actions, and with the concept of variable law the judicial side could become more and more the center of power. This could well be called "the imperial judiciary." Cut away from its true foundation, the power of the Court is nothing more than the instrument of unlimited power.[4]

It is important to realize here that Schaeffer sounded the alarm, stating:

The danger in regard to the rise of authoritarian government is that Christians will be still as long as their own religious activities, evangelism, and life-styles are not disturbed.

We are not excused from speaking, just because the culture and society no longer rest as much as they once did on Christian thinking. Moreover, Christians do not need to be in the majority in order to influence society.[5]

I and others heard that alarm. And from that point on, many of us became dedicated to changing society through an active Christian commitment—including many Christian lawyers fighting in the courts.

Everyone Can Do Something

With the publication in 1978 of *Whatever Happened to the Human Race?*, co-authored by Francis Schaeffer and United States Surgeon-General C. Everett Koop, the entire complexion of Protestant Christianity began to change. This in-depth discussion of abortion, infanticide, and euthanasia challenged Protestant Christianity, at that time a slumbering giant, to take a clear stand on this most crucial of issues. Until that point, virtually no one within the evangelical community was even discussing the sanctity of human life, let alone actively defending it. Abortion was still characterized as a "Catholic issue."

Schaeffer's book, accompanied by a five-part film series featuring Schaeffer and Dr. Koop, jarred Protestant Christians out of their ignorance and apathy and into social activism. The book has sold over two hundred thousand copies, and more than thirty-six thousand people viewed the film series during its first three-month tour in 1979. Thousands more have viewed it since then, on college campuses, in church and civic groups, as well as on special television broadcasts on both Christian and secular stations.

It would be impossible to measure the total impact of the book and the film series. But wherever I go within the prolife movement—at crisis pregnancy centers, in homes for unwed mothers, in adoption agencies, in the courts, on picket lines in front of abortion clinics, in social action groups—I constantly hear people say that they became involved as a direct result of Schaeffer's books and films exposing the slaughter of unborn, innocent life. Undoubtedly there are thousands who have become involved—in saving the unborn and caring for mothers and babies in need—as a result of Schaeffer's work. But more important than this are the untold numbers of little ones who are alive today because someone was willing to take a stand for their own life.

Perhaps the most challenging contribution Schaeffer made to the prolife movement was his own example and the belief that *everyone* could do something. He particularly challenged lawyers to go into the courts and take the offense in defense of life. But *everyone* can do something—whether it is voting for prolife candidates, picketing, street counseling, adoption, caring for unwed mothers, or committing oneself daily to fight through prayer in the spiritual battle between life and death. Although striken with cancer, from 1978 onward Schaeffer made frequent trips to Washington to meet with government officials—including Supreme Court Justices and officials in the White House, continually seeking to influence government to put an end to policies which destroy the sanctity of life. But he knew the other side of the battle too, as over the years Francis and Edith took many unwed mothers into their own home, or as he walked the picketline in front of a hospital which performed abortions just one month after he lay close to death with terminal cancer.

A Bombshell in the Evangelical Church

With the publication of *A Christian Manifesto* in 1981, Schaeffer made his strongest call for active Christian resistance to the oppressive acts of government, not only in totalitarian countries, but also in Western nations. I had met Schaeffer a year earlier through his son, Franky, and out of our talks together the concept for my own book *The Second American Revolution* was developed. This book, written eight years after studying Schaeffer's work, was inspired by his writings, and was a direct extension of Schaeffer's thought in the field of law. In addition to this, Schaeffer also wrote the foreword and served as one of the editors. It was during this time that the idea for *A Christian Manifesto* also took shape, and at Schaeffer's request I served as a researcher for the book.

In calling for Christian resistance to tyranny Schaeffer wrote:

> God has ordained the state as a *delegated* authority; it is not autonomous. The state is to be an agent of justice, to restrain evil by punishing the wrongdoer, and to protect the good in society. When it does the reverse, *it has no proper authority.* It is then a usurped authority and as such it becomes lawless and is tyranny. . . . The bottom line is that at a certain point there is not only the right, but the duty, to disobey the state.[6]

A Christian Manifesto dropped like a bombshell on the evangelical church. Some were not prepared to accept its bold message, and criticized Schaeffer for his activist stand. But for a growing number is was the catalyst which resulted in a complete commitment to Christian activism. Christians could no longer stand on the sidelines. Either they had to resist tyrannical acts or they would be condoning them. Standing silently and watching unborn children being murdered, or permitting the persecution of fellow Christians was the same as *helping* those who were actually committing these acts.

A Continuing Legacy

The full impact of Francis Schaeffer's activist approach has yet to be felt. Many young people presently coming through the education systems—including many who are now in law school—have read the works of Francis Schaeffer and others like him and are taking his activist approach toward law and government seriously. A few years ago, when a young woman asked me for advice about the possibility of her attending law school, I emphasized to her that she must go with the purpose of learning *how to use this to help change the world for Christ.* This then is a legacy of Francis Schaeffer—our calling as Christians to integrate our faith and our profession, our faith and *all* facets of life, so that the Lordship of Christ and His absolute laws are made manifest in the world around us.

As an example of how profound and expansive Francis Schaeffer's influence is, I would mention the Rutherford Institute. Schaeffer, of course, was a primary force in my founding the Institute. Briefly, the Institute is a nonprofit legal organization which defends Christians and other religious people who are persecuted by the state or by private individuals for practicing their religious and moral convictions. The Institute handles between twenty and thirty cases on a continuing basis. Our national office in northern Virginia is staffed full-time by a group of highly qualified lawyers and administrative personnel. The Institute also has a growing network of state chapters to expand its legal services nationwide. Since the Institute's inception in 1982, the number of affiliated attorneys has grown to approximately one hundred who take a strong activist stance, as well as hundreds more who are in some way involved in or influenced by the work of the Institute. In providing the basic impetus for the Institute—in his view of the law and in his call for Christians to take a clear stand on the crucial issues of the day—the impact of Schaeffer's work has been multiplied many times over.

A Clear and Costly Stand

In evaluating Francis Schaeffer's impact, he is probably criticized most frequently for not being a scholar. But this is to forget that the great men of history seldom set themselves up as great scholars. It is interesting to note that Jesus' disciples were not scholars—simply men of integrity and compassion who held to the truth and acted out that truth to influence the world for Jesus Christ.

Francis Schaeffer's impact on the practice of law by Christians surely equals that of many legal scholars. By standing firm on the truth of the Scriptures, and by taking a clear and costly stand on the crucial issues of the day, Schaeffer has deeply influenced the direction of law in this country. Moreover, we should not forget that many of those who opposed Jesus, such as the Pharisees, were in their time considered scholars. Their impact, however, was essentially negative. The world would be much better if we had more Francis Schaeffers and fewer modern Pharisees.

Schaeffer's influence, however, changed lives, and continues to change lives today. He left us the challenge to take hold of our responsibility to ensure that men stay free. As he said in *A Christian Manifesto*: "It is the responsibility of those holding this view to show it to be unique (the truth of total reality) for individual salvation and for society—by life, and by action."[7]

"[In the context of Hindu thought], Francis Schaeffer's teaching that there are 'no little people' can cause an explosion in your inner self giving you . . . the courage to dream new dreams, and the strength to step out in faith to realize those dreams."

Vishal Mangalwadi

Vishal Mangalwadi is the leader of a major movement among the peasant farmers of India to secure relief from spiritual and political oppression, and from economic exploitation. His work has already helped peasant farmers save hundreds of millions of rupees, while future plans include a massive national demonstration mobilizing 500,000 peasant farmers. He is the president of the Society for Service to Peasants, and is also active in the leadership of other theological, social, and political organizations. Mangalwadi holds a Master's degree in philosophy, and is the author of *The World of Gurus* and *Truth and Social Reform*. He and his wife, Ruth, who is actively involved in the work, live with their two daughters in New Delhi, India.

Chapter Twelve

Truth and Oppression

by
Vishal Mangalwadi
The Third World

Editor's Introduction and Background

The work of Vishal Mangalwadi among the rural peasants of India was something which Francis Schaeffer often mentioned with great appreciation. Dr. Schaeffer saw this as a remarkable example of how an individual Christian, living under the Lordship of Christ, can have a radical impact both upon individuals and his society, even under the most adverse spiritual and economic conditions.

I know that Vishal Mangalwadi would be reluctant to have himself and his work held up as an example. Nevertheless, it is important to know something about his personal background and his work—both as a means of seeing the significance of Dr. Schaeffer's influence, and as a challenge to Christians in the West to see the power of the gospel to transform individuals and to reach out and touch every area of human life.

Mangalwadi was born in a Quaker family from a high caste Indian background. He holds a Master's degree in philosophy, and has written *The World of Gurus*, a book on contemporary Indian gurus which has been widely acclaimed in India and abroad. While studying Western philosophy in the late 1960s, he went through a period of deep questioning. In his search for truth, he read Dr. Schaeffer's book *Escape from Reason*, which had been given to him a few years earlier. At the same time he began reading the Bible, and soon came to believe that the Bible was God's Word and the truth he had been seeking. In coming to this realization, Mangalwadi points out that *Escape from Reason* was a crucial influence which helped provide the framework for him to resolve his philosophical and other questions and to affirm the Scriptures as the Word of God. In the early 1970s, he wrote to Dr. Schaeffer about the possibility of coming to study at L'Abri. Dr. Schaeffer encouraged him to come, provided that he would supply his own means for getting there and for returning to India. As a direct answer to prayer, and through a series of remarkable events, the means were in fact provided. Mangalwadi went to L'Abri in 1973 to study and work for six months.

Although he was invited to remain as a L'Abri worker, Mangalwadi decided to return to India in order to serve and minister to his own people. The results of that decision were described recently in a monograph entitled *Indian Spirituality* by the Indian writer Prabhu Guptara. Guptara writes that with his credentials,

> Mangalwadi could have taken up work in academics, administration, or other fields, and found himself on a lovely career escalator. He chose, instead, to go back to his ancestral village to work for the upliftment of his people.
>
> His naive desire to do good was rudely shaken as he rapidly discovered that the age-old problems of caste, superstition, belief in black magic, illiteracy, disease and exploitation are now compounded by the increasing gap between the rich and the poor, even in rural India. He has been arrested, he has been beaten, his life has been threatened by different groups, because of his devotion to the Lord Jesus and his desire to work for the good of his people.[1]

Mangalwadi's commitment to Christ and to serving his people has resulted in the founding of a number of practical programs and organizations to implement these goals. In 1974 he helped found the *Theological Research and Communication In-*

stitute (TRACI). Located in New Delhi, TRACI conducts research and seminars, publishes a journal, has a practical outreach to people in need, while also meeting for daily prayer and worship. The members live and work together as a community without receiving any salary. Believing that "Jesus [is] the hope of India,. . . [they have] committed themselves to applying the Christian faith to the whole spectrum of Indian life."[2]

In 1976 Mangalwadi and his wife, Ruth, moved to a peasant village and, along with seven other Christians, began the *Association for Comprehensive Rural Assistance* (ACRA). The ACRA members also lived as a community on a subsistence level, providing practical assistance to the impoverished peasant farmers of the village, as part of their loving witness to Christ. Their work, however, was a direct challenge to the controlling political forces and to the local wing of the Communist Party of India. In November of 1984 they joined forces inciting a mob of one hundred men, armed with shotguns, axes, and spears, to attack the ACRA farm and buildings, setting them on fire, injuring a number of the ACRA members, taking everything of value, and destroying the ACRA ambulance, tractor, warehouses and stores. Many, including women and children, were burned and beaten, though no lives were lost. Although many in the mob were known to be ACRA members and could be identified, the local authorities have refused to take any action against them. Partly due to this kind of harassment and oppression, Vishal and Ruth found it necessary to leave the village with their two children and return to New Delhi.

With the founding in 1983 of the Society for Service to Peasants (*Kisan Sewa Samiti*—KSS), Mangalwadi's work has taken on national significance. Because of political corruption, government control, and exploitation by powerful interests, peasant farmers are forced to sell their grain and other farm products at less than what they cost to produce. Often this will happen year after year until they are pushed to the edge of survival and forced off their land. KSS was started to help change this situation by reforming the market system through creative alternatives. One of these alternatives includes the provision of warehousing and short-term loans so that peasant farmers are not forced to sell below cost at harvest time, but can wait until prices increase six months later. During September through November of 1985 this program helped farmers in one area earn an additional 125,000 rupees. (One rupee equals about $.09.) However, as those in power have become aware of the program, they have moved to protect their own interests by pressuring the banks and cutting off the sources for peasants to get term loans. To counteract this, Vishal has helped develop a program called *Indian Ground Works Trust*—a program which provides a channel for Westerners to invest in an Indian trust fund which then loans these funds on a short-term basis to Indian peasant farmers so that they can warehouse their farm products until they can sell them at a fair return. With sufficient support, the kind of savings mentioned above could be extended to many thousands of peasant farmers.[3]

In another effort, Mangalwadi helped initiate and organize a protest in 1984 involving three thousand farmers against a 235 percent increase in the government irrigation tariff. The successful protest resulted in an annual savings to farmers of four hundred million rupees.

The success of this effort has led Mangalwadi and others working with him to begin to organize a massive, nationwide protest against unjust fertilizer prices—prices which are more than double what is paid in neighboring countries and which have contributed to the further impoverishment of peasant farmers. As Mangalwadi explains in a recent newsletter, the success of this program will mean that

> the poor in India will save 12 billion rupees a year. This money will be ploughed back into the rural economy. But the problem is that the powerful will lose that amount. So a confrontation with powers and principalities is inevitable. . . . Is it coincidence that the Lord has opened a marvelous door and made me the head of the Peasants [commission] of the Janata Party (the main opposition party in India) at the national level?. . . My task is to draft the Agricultural Policy for the Janata Party, as well as to organize

farmers for exerting pressure for a just economic system in India. To insure just prices for fertilizer, we need to organize a minimum of 500,000 farmers. . . .

The battle for just prices for fertilizers has become as much a spiritual issue for some of us [here in India] as abortion is for some of our friends in the West. This is because another year of direct involvement with an oppressive political system and exploitative economic system has deepened my conviction that the Bible is true—we live in the kingdom of Satan. . . . [These] political evils have a diabolical dimension.[4]

The far-reaching scope and impact of Mangalwadi's work[5] have left him open to misunderstanding and criticism from many Christians in India. Some have not understood his emphasis that Christ must be the Lord of all life—including the social and political spheres—and would rather see a more "spiritual" approach. At the same time, his work should be distinguished from what Dr. Schaeffer called the "socialistic mentality"[6] which is being advanced by the evangelical left in the West. As summarized by Prabhu Guptara, the work of Mangalwadi, and others with him, is making a unique contribution—spiritually and socially—to the poor of India:

Willingness to suffer is understood and even lauded by most Christians. However, they have so far found it difficult to understand Mangalwadi's prayerful concern for the politics of the area and of the country, and his willingness to understand them, and be involved in them. . . . He does not believe that the political processes of India have been damaged beyond repair, or that they ought to be abandoned by Christians. On the contrary, he believes that politics are too important to be taken less than seriously by all those who wish to see an improvement in the conditions of life in the country. . . .

Strangely enough, this socially, politically and economically concerned citizen is an evangelist and preacher who . . . believes in a supernatural and interventionist God of Love and Justice. When I last met him a year ago, he and his wife and two children, after a working life spanning some fourteen years, owned little more than the clothes they stood up in. . . .

Mangalwadi is not the only Indian Christian of this sort. But there are not too many people like him. If India is to have a future, it must rest on such devotion, exertion and sacrifice, such utter trust and continual guidance from God in the everyday struggle for justice, equality, and true development.[7]

With this background in mind, Vishal Mangalwadi tells his own story below explaining how specific themes in Francis Schaeffer's life and work have influenced him in specific ways in his own work.

Lane T. Dennis

There is a saying in Hindi, India's major language, which states: "The oven cannot be heated for one single grain." This saying is commonly used to put down anyone who tries to take some new initiative. It means that no individual man is important, that he can do nothing of significance.

No Little People, No Little Places
If you grow up in an environment that conditions you to think that you are only a "little man," of no particular consequence, this idea becomes deeply ingrained in your own thinking. In this context, Francis Schaeffer's teaching that there are "no little people"[8] can cause an explosion in your inner self—giving you a new self-image, the courage to dream new dreams, and the strength to step out in faith to realize those dreams.

The self-confidence generated by this new outlook may move

you to seek recognition and importance for yourself. But Dr. Schaeffer also emphasized that there are "no little places." In other words, with God no place is unimportant, irrespective of how insignicant our world may consider it to be. And because there are "no little places" with God we have a reason and the strength to choose positions of seeming insignificance and powerlessness. When these two concepts are combined—that is, when the man of inner strength chooses a "small" position—the result can have a deep impact upon society because it is the opposite way of the world.

In my own life these two concepts have played a central role in how God has led me in making my own choices. When I went to L'Abri in 1973, I already felt that God wanted me to go to a small village in my ancestral area just to be a witness to the fact that He is there. (I had already turned down offers for teaching posts in a secular university and a theological college, as well as a leadership position in a multinational Christian organization.) My parents, who had prayed for years for this part of India, were against my going there because they could not see how I could survive financially in an economy where the hardest working peasant cannot feed his children. My parents could not imagine what kind of service an impractical graduate of philosophy could offer to illiterate peasants.

The Christian world of which I was a part was also against my going to a remote, inaccessible, primitive village. Many of my friends saw the move not merely as a waste of my talents, but also as an un-Biblical strategy. The "Urban Mission" emphasis had just been injected into Indian evangelical circles. Didn't Paul concentrate on big cities, on the centers of power, learning and influence? How then could I reject doors that were open for ministry among the influential, and instead choose a small place that offered no position, no job description, no salary? There were doubts in my own mind too. Could I enter a pioneer field alone, without a mission board to back me up, and still hope to build something out of practically nothing?

What I heard and saw at L'Abri was a clear confirmation of my decision. On one occasion Dr. Schaeffer spoke of "the mighty ways in which God used a dead stick" in the hand of

Moses, bringing life-giving water out of solid rock. As Dr. Schaeffer explained,

> Though we are limited and weak in talent, physical energy, and psychological strength, we are not less than a stick of wood. . . . Much can come from little if the little is truly concentrated to God. There are no little people and no big people in the true spiritual sense, but only consecrated and unconsecrated people.[9]

This message was liberating because it was Truth rooted in the Biblical view of God and man. It would have been just another sermon if it had come from someone else. But Dr. Schaeffer really believed that little people were significant. Each time I met him he would greet me kindly and respectfully. He lived by his principle that people mattered. Therefore when *he* said it, it had power.

But more important for me at that time was what Dr. Schaeffer said next:

> But if a Christian is consecrated, does this mean he will be in a big place instead of a little place? The answer, the next step, is very important: as there are no little people in God's sight, so there are no little places. To be wholly committed to God in the place where God wants him—this is the creature glorified.[10]

This truth, more than anything else, decided the matter for me. L'Abri itself asked me to become a helper. I agreed, but the Lord said "No." So I returned to India and moved to a farm in the middle of "nowhere"—to a 5' x 7' room with nothing else, no bathroom, no kitchen, no phone, no neighbors, no organization, no co-worker. Almost eighteen months prior to this move I had proposed marriage to Ruth, and she had declined. But two weeks after I moved into the jungle, her letter of consent came. That was the first blessing of obedience. Together the Lord blessed us with two daughters, and a ministry that has taken the form of two organizations engaged in evangelism, discipling, development, and reform. It now seems that three new dimensions are being added to the ministry: influencing the world of ideas through writing and lecturing; influencing the political process in India through a peasant movement; and tackling poverty and unemployment through industry and business. The ministry itself is geared to reach people who are little and powerless from the world's perspective, but in the process the Lord has used it to touch some "big" people too.

Ash Heap Lives

Another factor which helped me choose life with the peasants was Dr. Schaeffer's teaching on the place of material possessions. He stressed, for example, that the supernatural perspective on life does not square up with the practice of materialism—that is, of laying up treasures on earth. This he called "living ash heap lives," or spending "most of our time and money for things that will end up in the city dump."[11] Jesus said that giving earthly treasures to the poor was the way to accumulate treasures in heaven. This, Dr. Schaeffer insisted, had to be taken literally:

> The Bible tells us that a cause-and-effect relationship exists between what happens now and what happens in eternity. We are often told, "You can't take it with you." But this is not true. You can take it with you—if you are a Christian. The question is, Will we?[12]

In addition to this Dr. Schaeffer stressed that

> The Scripture makes no distinction between giving to the needy and giving to missionary work. Often to the evangelical mind, money given to missions is the only money given to the Lord. Now, I am not minimizing contributing to missionary work. Christians do not do this enough. But there is also a practical humanitarianism in the Scripture. Christians have the

important job of meeting men's material needs as well as their personal and spiritual needs.[13]

When we live at a physical distance from the poor, it is easy to limit our giving to a budgeted amount. But when we live with the poor, and take this teaching seriously, then we can't budget giving. Jesus' command, "sell all that ye have, and give alms" takes on a new urgency. Ruth once had to go as far as giving away her wedding ring to help a brother get married—because we neither had the money to buy him a ring nor anything which we could sell to buy it. However, to our pleasant surprise, we have discovered in our lives another Biblical principle which is also true—that we receive one hundredfold for what we sacrifice for Christ. Ruth and I have repeatedly had the joy of giving our all, but we have lacked nothing. As we have sought to practice Dr. Schaeffer's teaching on "simple life-style," we have in fact seen God's abundance.

Sitting in the "Supernatural Chair"

One night as we were finishing dinner in our rural community, the chief of the village Karri drove in on a scooter and asked, "Do any of you know sorcery? A woman in my village has been bitten by a cobra. We have given her medical help as well as brought in the best sorcerers from neighboring villages, but she has become unconscious and is dying."

"We don't know sorcery," I replied, "but we pray."

"Please come and pray," he pleaded. We agreed to come and pray, and we left with the chief.

I took along two other Christians, as well as a Muslim who had been a hardened criminal. I had met him in prison on one of the few occasions when I have been arrested. He had been locked up with his gang for eighteen months on several charges of murder, robbery, and other serious crimes. His gang, however, was so powerful that no one dared to witness against them, and eventually they were all acquitted. Soon after, he left his gang and moved in with our community. I took him along that night as a bodyguard because Ruth feared that the whole story of the snake and the woman might simply be a trap to get me out at night in order to kidnap or kill me.

When we arrived there were more than fifty people, including a doctor, crowded in the room around the woman's bed. They showed us the marks of the snake's fangs on her foot. She seemed dead and did not respond even when pinched.

I had seen many answers to prayers of all kinds, but never had I faced a situation like this. My faith was on trial before fifty Hindus—sorcerers on one side, a medical doctor on the other, and a Muslim criminal with me. I remembered the "two chairs" Dr. Schaeffer talked about at the end of *Death in the City*: on one hand, the chair of a scientific materialist, who does not believe that God exists and/or can act into the material world; and on the other hand, the chair of a Christian, who believes that God not only exists but that the mechanistic universe is open to God's intervention—that God can and does act in the material world.

Rarely have I prayed a more carefully reasoned prayer than on that occasion. As we knelt down to close our eyes in prayer, with a crowd of Hindus and Muslims looking on, I took my seat very consciously in the "supernatural chair." I thanked God that He was there. I thanked Him for being greater than the snake and its poison, greater than magic and modern medicine. I praised Him because He made the human body and He knows how it works and how it can be repaired when it breaks down. I thanked Him for sending me into this area of darkness to make me a witness that He was there. I asked God to demonstrate that night that He was this woman's Creator, and that Jesus loved her and her family so much that He died for them.

By the time we opened our eyes, she had opened hers too. When I asked her name, she replied, "Ramkali." Everyone was stunned into silence and awe. But my Muslim friend, who is usually a quiet person, was very excited. I had not noticed that he too had knelt down near the bed along with the three of us Christians. He held my hand tightly and said, "This is the first time in my life that I have prayed. Now I know that God is real."

The Kingdoms of This World
One striking difference between Dr. Schaeffer and other great evangelical preachers was that while most preachers seemed horrified by sin, Dr. Schaeffer seemed equally horrified at the prospect of political totalitarianism. He often preached against

it. In fact, to some it seemed that he was turning the Christian's attention more toward political freedom than to personal holiness. For years I was not sure if it was Biblical to give this matter the kind of importance Dr. Schaeffer had. As far as I know, he did not give an extensive Biblical basis for taking the issue of totalitarianism so seriously. Therefore, I do not blame those Christians who do not share Dr. Schaeffer's fear of Russian totalitarianism and his advocacy of military preparedness in defense of peace and freedom. However, I have recently begun to look at the question of totalitarianism and political oppression in a new way. In struggling with political and bureaucratic corruption in India, I found myself getting arrested for what I considered rather mild protests against injustices in our society. As I faced police officials who threatened to kill me, and as I discovered plots to kill me, hatched by the politicians of the ruling party, I began to understand what the New Testament means by "the kingdom of Satan."

But it was a Hindu film, *Ardha Satya* (Half Truth), which the Lord finally used to remove the scales from my eyes. The film shows a police inspector in Bombay who fights the political and bureaucratic corruption in his own department with great dignity. But in the end he destroys not the evil but himself. The film's point is that courage and integrity are "half truths"; or in other words, in our system evil is greater than good. Neither the brave police officer, nor the journalist, nor the trade unionist, nor the civil liberties activist, nor even the social scientist understands the social evil. The film director himself does not pretend to understand. As I sat and watched the helplessness and powerlessness of these brave and honest people in the face of the all-pervasive evil in our society, I jumped out of my seat and said to Ruth, "Of course, there is no way that they can understand social evil. It has a diabolical dimension to it which they just rule out."

In the temptation of Jesus, Satan claimed that the world's kingdoms—that is, the political and economic institutions of this world—were his (Luke 4:5, 6). Jesus acknowledged Satan to be the prince of this world (John 14:30). Thus Satan is out to possess not merely the souls of men, but their political and economic institutions as well. When we think of political and economic institutions as "secular" and "religiously neutral," we indeed sit on the chair of the philosophical materialist. Because the universe is a supernatural reality, it is not possible to build a "secular" state which leaves God or Satan out of the picture. As Dr. Schaeffer stressed, the Lordship of Christ must encompass the *whole* of life, including our political life. The gospel of the kingdom of God is a challenge to the kingdom of Satan—that is, to the oppressive, exploitative, and dehumanizing institutions of men.

What begins as sin at an individual level indeed culminates in hell in eternity. But here in this life, it culminates in slavery. Salvation and holiness, on the other hand, culminate in freedom. On rereading the New Testament, I have become convinced that the Bible is indeed as much concerned with issues of freedom from slavery and totalitarianism as it is with being saved from hell. The former is the result of sin in this life and the latter is the consequence of sin in eternity. Again, I think it was Dr. Schaeffer's great contribution that he pointed out that initially sin was not a matter of *behavior* but of *belief*—of turning away from truth and believing in a false God. Sin is "theological prostitution." Therefore, the first commandments of the law deal with believing in the true God. What we believe—that is, our ideas—determine where our society and history will end up. Our basic presuppositions about God and reality have practical consequences.

Ten years ago Ruth and I started struggling with poverty, illiteracy, unemployment, ill health, suppression of women, and other evils, at the micro-level of action and projects. The action against poverty is continuing and expanding, but the realities of poverty have driven us back to presuppositions, to the ideas and morals that drive our people into slavery. We have become all the more convinced that it is not possible to build up a movement for economic development and reform from the grass roots without infusing a new outlook regarding the significance of each little individual. People will not act unless they believe that they are significant, that their choices, their voices, their actions matter; that they *can* affect history. Creation of new ideas, new industries, new institutions is seriously inhibited until the emphasis is put on the creativity itself—until we see the universe as a creation of God, and man as a creative being. If a society believes that the universe is not a "creation," but a "projection" of "Universal Consciousness" (Maya or Brahma), then what society will cultivate is not the forces of human creativity but the power of meditation or yoga. One reason why we in India have failed to create wealth in the previous centuries is that our best minds spent a lifetime cultivating the power of meditation rather than creativity.

In a society built largely on distrust, dishonesty, and corruption, a life of daily, habitual commitment to righteousness and to opposing social evil is not possible *unless we believe that we live in a moral universe* where a final dichotomy between good and evil does exist. Right is *not* wrong, and wrong is *not* right—in business or politics or "transcendence." Hinduism does not provide the strength to suffer for righteousness because it does not see morals as absolutes, nor does it affirm a final victory of good over evil.

The problem of India's poverty is not rooted merely in its ancient beliefs and practices. Our greatest contemporary problem is that the state does not believe in God, and therefore it has to set itself up as the "savior." It defines salvation in terms of industrialization and economic development. The "Five Year Plan" is lifted up as the way of "salvation." Such grand plans require large financial investments which are raised at the expense of the poor masses who presently produce what little wealth there is. This exploitation of the poor by the state is "sanctified" with slogans like "mobilization of financial resources for economic development." The poor in India suffer not because they are illiterate, hungry, or sick, but because they live in an intellectual, political, and economic system which is exploitative and oppressive—because they live in the kingdom of Satan. They are poor because our system is committed to *keep* them poor. In this context, "development" is a powerless concept. To meet the challenge of poverty we need the kind of reformation which Dr. Schaeffer talked about—a radical transformation of both our ideas and our institutions.

Our experience of the hard realities of India has reinforced Dr.

Schaeffer's teaching that true freedom and lasting prosperity can be built only on the rock of God's Word. In our quest to relieve oppression and to realize justice in the Third World, we will have offered a fitting tribute to Dr. Schaeffer only when we come to terms with the truth concerning supernatural and moral reality which he so often emphasized—that Jesus, not Caesar, is the Prince of Peace.

Chronology

1912   Francis August Schaeffer was born on January 30 in Germantown, Pennsylvania. He was the only child of Francis August Schaeffer III and Bessie Williamson Schaeffer.

1914   Edith Rachel Merritt Seville (Francis Schaeffer's future wife) was born in China on November 3. She was the fourth child of George Hugh Seville and Jessie Maude Merritt Seville.

1930   Schaeffer became a Christian at the age of eighteen after reading the Bible, beginning with Genesis, for about six months.

1932   Met his future wife on June 26 at the First Presbyterian Church of Germantown, Pennsylvania.

1935   Graduated from Hampden-Sydney College in June. Schaeffer was second in his senior class and graduated *magna cum laude*.

1935   Married Edith Seville on July 26.

1935   Entered Westminster Theological Seminary in September.

1937   The Schaeffers' first daughter, Priscilla was born on June 18.

1938   Schaeffer graduated from Faith Theological Seminary, which he had helped to found after a split with Westminster in 1937.

1938   Ordained as the first pastor in the Bible Presbyterian denomination, and began serving as pastor of Covenant Presbyterian Church in Grove City, Pennsylvania.

1941   Elected moderator of the Great Lakes Presbytery of the Bible Presbyterian Church.

1941   Began serving as associate pastor of the Bible Presbyterian Church in Chester, Pennsylvania.

1941   The Schaeffers' second daughter, Susan, was born on May 28.

1943   Began serving as the pastor of the Bible Presbyterian Church in St. Louis, Missouri.

1945   The Schaeffers' third daughter, Deborah, was born on May 3.

1947   Traveled throughout Europe for three months to evaluate the state of the church in Europe as a representative of the Independent Board for Presbyterian Foreign Missions and as the American Secretary for the Foreign Relations Department of the American Council of Christian Churches.

1948   Moved to Lausanne, Switzerland with Edith and their three daughters to be missionaries to Europe. Their work primarily involved the Children for Christ ministry, and helping with the formation of the International Council of Christian Churches.

1949   Moved to Chalet des Fr[e]nes in the mountain village of Champéry, Switzerland.

1951   Went through a spiritual crisis in the winter months. During this time, Schaeffer recognized that something was deeply wrong and he carefully reconsidered his Christian commitment and the priorities in his life. Schaeffer emerged from this experience with a new certainty about his faith, a new emphasis on sanctification and the work of the Holy Spirit, and a new direction in his life which would unfold over the next four years.

1952   Francis August Schaeffer IV was born on August 3.

1953   Returned to the U.S. with family on furlough.

1953- Traveled across the country speaking 346 times during
1954   515 days about the deeper spiritual life. During this time Schaeffer first presented the talks which grew out of his spiritual crisis and later became the basis for his book *True Spirituality*.

1954   Awarded honorary Doctor of Divinity degree in May by Highland College in Long Beach, California.

1954   Returned to Champéry, Switzerland in September. Franky Schaeffer contracted polio on the boat en route to Switzerland.

1955   Received notice from the Swiss government on February 14 that they must leave Switzerland permanently within six weeks.

1955   The Schaeffers moved into Chalet les Mélèzes in Huémoz, Switzerland on April 1 after receiving the money needed to purchase les Mélèzes through a series of miraculous circumstances.

1955 Resigned from the Independent Board for Presbyterian Foreign Missions on June 4, marking the informal beginning of L'Abri Fellowship.

1955- Francis Schaeffer, along with Edith, led the work of
1984 L'Abri as the primary focus of their lives, up until shortly before Dr. Schaeffer's death.

1958 English L'Abri is founded after Schaeffer gave lectures at Oxford and elsewhere in England.

1968 Published *The God Who Is There*, the first of his twenty-three books, based on lectures given at Wheaton College in 1965.

1971 Received honorary Doctor of Letters degree in June from Gordon College in Wenham, Massachusetts.

1974 Began work on the book and film for *How Should We Then Live?* with Franky Schaeffer.

1977 Began a twenty-two-city seminar and speaking tour in January for the film series *How Should We Then Live?*

1977 Helped to found the International Council on Biblical Inerrancy.

1977 Began work on the film series *Whatever Happened to the Human Race?* with C. Everett Koop and Franky Schaeffer.

1978 Diagnosed as having lymphoma cancer in October, at Mayo Clinic in Rochester, Minnesota.

1979   Began a national seminar and speaking tour in September for the film series *Whatever Happened to the Human Race?*

1979   The American headquarters of L'Abri was established in Rochester, Minnesota.

1982   Publication of *The Complete Works of Francis A. Schaeffer* in July.

1983   Received honorary Doctor of Laws degree from the Simon Greenleaf School of Law.

1983   Was flown in critical condition from Switzerland to Mayo Clinic in December.

1984   Went on a seminar tour to ten Christian colleges during March and April in connection with his last book, *The Great Evangelical Disaster*.

1984   Died in his home in Rochester, Minnesota on May 15.

Books by
Francis A. Schaeffer

The following list includes all twenty-five books written by Francis A. Schaeffer;[1] two of these were coauthored and one was compiled posthumously from his letters. All except the last two in the list below are available in *The Complete Works of Francis A. Schaeffer* (Westchester, Ill.: Crossway Books, 1982; second edition, 1985) as revised and edited by Dr. Schaeffer in 1980 and 1981. Those with initials after the title are still in print from the original publishers. (See below for each publisher's full name and address.) The books are arranged below according to the five volume division of *The Complete Works* (available only as a five volume set).

In *The Complete Works*, Volume I: *A Christian View of Philosophy and Culture*.

> *The God Who Is There*. IVP, 1968.
> *Escape From Reason*. IVP, 1968.
> *He Is There and He Is Not Silent*. TH, 1972.
> *Back to Freedom and Dignity*. 1972.

In *The Complete Works*, Volume II: *A Christian View of the Bible as Truth*.

Genesis in Space and Time. IVP, 1972.
No Final Conflict. 1975.
Joshua and the Flow of Biblical History. 1975.
Basic Bible Studies. TH, 1972.
Art and the Bible. IVP, 1973.

In *The Complete Works*, Volume III: *A Christian View of Spirituality*.

No Little People. IVP, 1974.
True Spirituality. TH, 1971.
The New Super-Spirituality. 1972.
Two Contents, Two Realities, 1974.

In *The Complete Works*, Volume IV: *A Christian View of the Church*.

The Church at the End of the Twentieth Century. CB, 1985 (1970).
The Church Before the Watching World. CB, 1985 (1971).
The Mark of the Christian. IVP, 1970.
Death in the City. 1969.
The Great Evangelical Disaster. CB, 1984.

In *The Complete Works*, Volume V: *A Christian View of the West*.

Pollution and the Death of Man. TH, 1970.
How Should We Then Live? CB, 1983 (1976).
Whatever Happened to the Human Race? (with C. Everett Koop). CB, 1983 (1979).
A Christian Manifesto. CB, 1981.

Two other books not included in *The Complete Works* are:

Everyone Can Know (with Edith Schaeffer). TH, 1973.

Letters of Francis A. Schaeffer (with Lane T. Dennis, ed.). CB, 1985.

Publishers' full names and addresses:

CB: Crossway Books, Westchester, IL 60153.
IVP: InterVarsity Press, Downers Grove, IL 60515.
TH: Tyndale House, Wheaton, IL 60187.

Books by
Edith Schaeffer

The following list includes all the books written by Edith Schaeffer, all of which are still in print. The first two give a biographical account of the lives of Francis and Edith Schaeffer as well as the work of L'Abri Fellowship.[1]

On the Schaeffers' lives and the work of L'Abri:

L'Abri. TH, 1969.
The Tapestry. WB, 1981.

On the Christian faith and life:

Hidden Art. TH, 1972.
Christianity Is Jewish. TH, 1975.
What Is a Family? FHR, 1975.
A Way of Seeing. FHR, 1977.
Affliction. FHR, 1978.
Everyone Can Know (with Francis A. Schaeffer).
    TH, 1973.
Lifelines. CB, 1982.
Common Sense Christian Living. TN, 1983.
Forever Music. TN, 1986.

Publishers' full names and addresses:

CB: Crossway Books, Westchester, IL 60153.
FHR: Fleming H. Revell, Old Tappan, NJ 07675.
TH: Tyndale House, Wheaton, IL 60187.
TN: Thomas Nelson, Nashville, TN 37214.
WB: Word Books, Waco, TX 76796.

Chalet les Mélèzes

About the Photographer

Sylvester Jacobs admits to learning photography in the "old school" way—by observing the craft firsthand with masters like Henri Cartier-Bresson and Tony Ray-Jones, and by doing it. With the encouragement of art historian Dr. Hans Rookmaaker, his compositional ability was also refined by detailed study of seventeenth-century Dutch paintings.

Jacobs's work has been exhibited in most major British cities, in Amsterdam, and in major U.S. cities. His work also appears in the permanent collection of The Victoria and Albert Museum in London.

Jacobs has contributed to the photographic content of several books, including *Portrait of England* and *The European Horse*. He also wrote and photographed *Born Black* (Hodder and Stoughton), *Portrait of a Shelter* (InterVarsity), and *Photography: A Practical Guide* (Nelson).

The photographs in this book were selected from a series taken of the Schaeffers, and of L'Abri Fellowship in Switzerland, from the early 1970s through the early 1980s. At the L'Abri community, Jacobs and his wife found spiritual affirmation, and encouragement in his work, as well as a deep relationship with Francis and Edith Schaeffer.

Jacobs lives with his wife and three daughters near London, England.

Notes

Introduction

1. Francis A. Schaeffer, *The Great Evangelical Disaster* in *The Complete Works of Francis A. Schaeffer*, Vol. IV, second ed. (Westchester, Ill.: Crossway Books, 1985), pp. 321, 322.

2. Throughout the book Francis Schaeffer is referred to in different ways by the various authors. No attempt was made to make these references uniform since it seemed better to leave these in the form with which the various authors were most comfortable. Thus some chapters usually refer to Francis Schaeffer as "Dr. Schaeffer" while others simply use "Schaeffer." This later form has been used in the introduction and other material written by the editor.

3. See further, Lane T. Dennis ed., *The Letters of Francis A. Schaeffer* (Westchester, Ill.: Crossway Books, 1985), esp. pp. 14 and 31-82.

4. Francis A. Schaeffer, *No Little People* in *The Complete Works of Francis A. Schaeffer*, Vol. I (Westchester, Ill.: Crossway Books, 1982), p. 8.

5. *Ibid.*, p. 14.

Chapter 2 / The Fragmentation and Integration of Truth

1. *The God Who Is There*, I, p. 12. Quotations from Schaeffer's works are taken from *The Complete Works of Francis A. Schaeffer*, 5 vols. (Westchester, Ill.: Crossway Books, 1982).

2. *Escape from Reason*, I, p. 211.

3. *The God Who Is There*, I, p. 43.

4. *Pollution and the Death of Man*, V, pp. 3-7.

5. As in *How Should We Then Live?*, V, and others.

6. *Ibid.*, pp. 114, 115.

7. *Ibid.*, pp. 107, 209.

8. *The God Who Is There*, I, pp. 38, 39.

9. C. S. Lewis, *An Experiment in Criticism* (Cambridge: Cambridge University Press, 1961), p. 25.

10. *Ibid.*, p. 139.

11. *Ibid.*, p. 138.

12. As he develops in *Art and the Bible*, II.

13. Charles Garside, *Zwingli and the Arts* (New Haven: Yale University Press, 1966), p. 171.

14. See his comments on Rembrandt and Bach in *How Should We Then Live?*, V, pp. 128, 132, 133.

15. Herbert N. Schneidau, *Sacred Discontent: The Bible and Western Tradition* (Berkeley: University of California Press, 1977).

16. *How Should We Then Live?*, V, p. 83.

17. See *Art and the Bible*, II, pp. 405-408.

18. Schaeffer is often accused of "rationalism," of relegating Christian faith to the dictates of human reason. Nothing could be further from the truth. Schaeffer clearly limits our knowledge of God to what He Himself reveals in Scripture, insisting that autonomous human beings can know nothing about God from their reason alone. By "rational," Schaeffer is referring to the realm of logical antithesis and to what we might think of as objective truth. See his explanations in the appendix to *The God Who Is There*, I, pp. 183-185.

19. *Ibid.*, p. 186.

20. Robert Solomon, quoted in *HIS*, October 1981, p. 6, from *Southwest Airlines Magazine*.

21. See *The God Who Is There*, I, pp. 103-105 and the quite sophisticated arguments about language, although couched in clear, nontechnical terminology, in *He Is There and He Is Not Silent*, I.

22. See *The God Who Is There*, I, pp. 129-142.

23. *Ibid.*, p. 187.

Chapter 3 / The Life of the Mind and the Way of Life

1. Francis A. Scheffer, *The God Who Is There* in *The Complete Works of Francis A. Schaeffer*, Vol. I, second ed. (Westchester, Ill.: Crossway Books, 1985), p. 186.

2. Schaeffer, *The God Who Is There* (Chicago: InterVarsity Press, 1968), p. 21. In this same passage in *The Complete Works*, Vol. I, p. 15, the last two sentences in my quotation have been dropped. This would seem to suggest that, in editing his earlier books for the *Complete Works*, Schaeffer modified his views on Kierkegaard somewhat, apparently in his later years, seeing Kierkegaard's separation of faith and reason in less absolute terms than he did in earlier years.

3. For arguments that support this claim, see further Arvin Vos, *Aquinas, Calvin and Contemporary Protestant Thought* (Grand Rapids, Mich.: Eerdmans, 1985).

4. Schaeffer, *Escape From Reason* in *The Complete Works*, Vol. I, pp. 209-211. Emphasis added.

5. Schaeffer, *The Great Evangelical Disaster* in *The Complete Works*, Vol. IV, second ed., pp. 317, 318.

6. Gordon Clark's outstanding history of Western philosophy suggests the wisdom of this approach. See Gordon Clark, *Thales to Dewey* (Boston: Houghton Mifflin, 1957), pp. 533, 534.

7. Schaeffer, *Escape* in *The Complete Works*, Vol. I, second ed., p. 15.

8. A parallel can be seen between Schaeffer's views on Aquinas and Kierkegaard. As with Aquinas, Schaeffer seems to say that Kierkegaard did not intend for his views to have led to where Schaeffer believes they did lead. Thus Schaeffer wrote:

> I do not think that Kierkegaard would be happy, or would agree, with that which has developed from his thinking in either secular or religious existentialism. But what he wrote gradually led to the absolute separation of the rational and logical from faith. . . . *But the important thing about him is that when he put forth the concept of a leap of faith, he became in a real way the father of all modern existential thought, both secular and theological.*

(See *The God Who Is There* in *The Complete Works*, Vol. I, p. 16.) Thus the point which Schaeffer intends to make is that a *principle* was introduced in "the concept of a leap of faith" which later bore bitter fruit.

9. See Brand Blanshard, *Reason and Belief* (London: Allen and Unwin, 1974), ch. 6. Blanshard, a professor of philosophy at Yale who was also an outspoken critic of Christianity, understood Kierkegaard in ways very close to Schaeffer's. For an even stronger reading of Kierkegaard as an irrationalist, see Alastair McKinnon, "Kierkegaard, 'Paradox' and Irrationalism," in *Essays on Kierkegaard*, ed. Jerry H. Gill (Minneapolis: Burgess, 1969), pp. 102-112. In an earlier work by the liberal theologian and philosopher L. Harold DeWolf, *The Religious Revolt Against Reason* (New York: Harper, 1949), DeWolf is extremely critical of the "revolt against reason" which he sees in Kierkegaard. Moreover, he argues that Barth, Brunner and Reinhold Niebuhr were directly influenced by Kierkegaard's works, and that there is a serious problem of irrationalism in their work which stems back to Kierkegaard. It is interesting to note that DeWolf's book was published at the time when Schaeffer probably first began to deal with these issues.

10. It is true that we probably understand both Aquinas and Kierkegaard better today and that we are able to recognize some shortcomings in Schaeffer's treatment of both. See further, Ronald Nash, *The Word of God and the Mind of Man* (Grand Rapids: Zondervan, 1982), p. 34 and Ronald Nash, *Christian Faith and Historical Understanding* (Grand Rapids: Zondervan, 1984), pp. 151, 152. See also Vos, *Aquinas, Calvin and Contemporary Protestant Thought* (cited in Note 3).

11. Nietzsche is notoriously difficult to understand, and I recognize the possibility that some may think that I have done the same thing with him that Schaeffer did with Kierkegaard. My reading of Nietzsche, however, is in line

with the respected interpretation of Walter Kaufmann in his book, *Nietzsche* (New York: World Publishing Co., 1950).

12. The full text from which I quote can be found on pages 95, 96 of *The Portable Nietzsche*, ed. Walter Kaufmann (New York: Viking Press, 1954).

13. Nietzsche, *Thus Spoke Zarathustra: First Part*, in *The Portable Nietzsche*, p. 171.

14. Nietzsche, *The Antichrist* in *The Portable Nietzsche*, p. 570.

15. *Thus Spoke Zarathustra*, p. 124.

16. *Thus Spoke Zarathustra*, pp. 126, 127.

17. According to numerous reports, Sartre converted to Catholicism before he died.

18. Schaeffer, *He is There and He is Not Silent* in *The Complete Works*, Vol. I, second ed., p. 279.

19. For further discussions along these lines, see: Ronald Nash, *Christianity and the Hellenistic World* (Grand Rapids: Zondervan, 1985); Ronald Nash, *Christian Faith and Historical Understanding* (Grand Rapids: Zondervan, 1984); and Ronald Nash, *The Word of God and the Mind of Man* (Grand Rapids: Zondervan, 1982).

Chapter 5 / The Glory and Ruin of Man

1. All quotations, unless indicated otherwise, are from Dr. Schaeffer's personal letters. Many of the same ideas are found in his books, especially *True Spirituality* (Wheaton, Ill.: Tyndale House, 1972).

2. *The Roots of Sorrow: Reflections on Depression and Hope* (Westchester, Ill.: Crossway Books, 1986). This book gives a much more detailed account of all the themes mentioned in this essay and demonstrates, for the layperson or the professional, how the insights of psychology and psychiatry may be tested within a Biblical framework, especially in the area of depression.

3. Anthony Clare, *Let's Talk About Me* (BBC, 1981), p. 238.

Chapter 6 / Francis Schaeffer and His Critics

1. For proponents of this view see for example: Richard V. Pierard, "The Unmaking of Francis Schaeffer: An Evangelical Tragedy," *The Wittenburg Door*, April-May 1984, pp. 27-31; and Ronald A. Wells, "Whatever Happened to Francis Schaeffer?," *The Reformed Journal*, May 1983, pp. 10-13.

2. As quoted in Stephen Board, "The Rise of Francis Schaeffer," *Eternity*, June 1977, p. 41.

3. From Ronald A. Wells, "Francis Schaeffer's Jeremiad: A Review Article," *The Reformed Journal*, May 1982, pp. 16-20. Cited subsequently as: Wells, "Jeremiad."

4. As quoted in Kenneth L. Woodward, "Guru of Fundamentalism," *Newsweek*, November 1, 1982, p. 88. It should be noted that Noll wrote to Schaeffer apologizing if the statement had caused Schaeffer embarrassment; at the same time, he explained that he had been quoted correctly though "out of context." Although Noll has expressed much appreciation for Schaeffer and

his work on other occasions, Schaeffer continued for his remaining years to see serious problems in Noll's views, and the converse is also true. The basic disagreement was never resolved. (See further, Note 8 below.) Jack Rogers makes the same point as Noll in "Francis Schaeffer: The Promise and the Problem (1)," *The Reformed Journal*, May 1977, p. 12-15; and the second part of this article appearing in *The Reformed Journal*, June 1977, pp. 15-19, esp. p. 18.

5. It seems curious that this kind of reaction seems to come mostly from academicians within evangelical colleges, rather than from evangelical academicians on the faculties of secular schools.

6. *Webster's New World Dictionary* (2nd college edition; New York: The World Publishing Company, 1972), p. 1274.

7. Woodward, p. 88.

8. After this quote appeared, a long series of correspondence ensued between Noll, Schaeffer and later historian George M. Marsden. This extended over eighteen months and included more than one hundred pages of letters and supporting materials. Though there was some movement on both sides, and perhaps a greater understanding of their differences, both sides remained convinced to the end that the opposing position was seriously mistaken.

9. See for example: Ralph Barton Perry, *Puritanism and Democracy* (New York: Vanguard, 1944); Perry G. Miller, *Errand into the Wilderness* (Cambridge, Mass.: Harvard University Press, 1956); and Sacvan Bercovitch, *The Puritan Origins of America* (New Haven, Conn.: Yale University Press, 1975).

10. See for example John Winthrop's sermon preached on board ship before even landing in the New World in 1630, where Winthrop proclaims: "Thus stands the cause betweene God and us. Wee are entered into Covenant with him for this worke,. . . for wee must Consider that wee shall be as a Citty upon a Hill, the eies of all people are uppon us. . ." Winthrop concludes by reciting the blessings and curses from the renewal of the Covenant ceremony in Deuteronomy 29 and 30. For the full text of the sermon see Robert N. Bellah, *The Broken Covenant: American Civil Religion in Time of Trial* (New York: Seabury Press, 1975), pp. 14, 15.

11. To be exact, this is George M. Marsden's term which he used first in his article "Quest for a Christian America," *Eternity*, May 1983, pp. 18-23. Noll apparently shares this view with Marsden since the article appeared (with some revisions) in the book which they coauthored along with Nathan O. Hatch entitled, *The Search for Christian America* (Westchester, Ill.: Crossway Books, 1983).

12. Francis A. Schaeffer, *The Great Evangelical Disaster* (Westchester, Ill.: Crossway Books, 1984), pp. 183, 184 (cited subsequently as: *GED*). This specific quote appeared after the appearance of Noll's quote in *Newsweek*; the ideas in this quote, however, have been presented in a number of places in Schaeffer's books going back to at least the mid-1970s.

13. Alexis de Tocqueville, *Democracy in America*, seventh ed., trans. John C. Spencer (New York: Edward Walker, 1847).

14. *Ibid.*, p. 337.

15. *Ibid.*, p. 333.

16. *Ibid.*, p. 334.

17. For a perceptive study of American culture today, especially in light of individualism and its relationship to American cultural traditions and practices, see Robert N. Bellah, *et al.*, *Habits of the Heart: Individualism and Commitment in American Life* (Berkeley, Calif.: University of California Press, 1985). This work is notable in that Bellah consciously patterned the study after Tocqueville's *Democracy in America*, taking the title from the phrase used by Tocqueville—i.e., "habits of the heart"—to describe the mores of the American people. Note especially Chap. 9, pp. 219-249 on religion in public life.

18. See Max Weber, *The Protestant Ethic and the Spirit of Capitalism*, trans. Talcott Parsons (New York: Charles Scribner's Sons, 1958).

19. Michael Novak's *The Spirit of Democratic Capitalism* (New York: Simon and Schuster, 1982) offers further insight concerning the influence of Christianity upon sociopolitical and economic systems.

20. This point was made succinctly by Alan Beasley in his review of Dale Vree's provocative book, *From Berkeley to Berlin and Back* (Nashville, Tenn.: Thomas Nelson, 1985). Beasley writes:

> The most obvious manifestation of this [cultural] revolution is its sexual aspect: over-the-counter pornography; abortion on demand; the gay lifestyle increasingly legitimized; decreasing respect for life-long, faithful marriage; raising children portrayed as a second-class occupation; and more. But the cultural revolution isn't limited to sexuality. . . . Its basic goal has been to legitimize a lifestyle of unbridled pleasure where anything goes as long as the old bromide about "consenting adults" is followed; and it has succeeded to an astounding degree.

In *Eternity*, February 1986, p. 42.

21. Francis A. Schaeffer, *GED*, p. 39.

22. Ronald A. Wells, "Whatever Happened to Francis Schaeffer?" *The Reformed Journal*, May 1983, pp. 11, 12. Cited subsequently as: Wells, "Whatever Happened."

23. Mark A. Noll, "When Bad Books Happen to Good Causes: A Review Article," *The Reformed Journal*, May 1984, p. 27. Cited subsequently as: Noll, "When Bad."

24. Francis A. Schaeffer, *How Should We Then Live?* in *The Complete Works*, Vol. IV (Westchester, Ill.: Crossway Books, 1982), p. 123. Cited subsequently as: Schaeffer, *HSWTL- CW, IV*.

25. *Ibid.*, p. 135.

26. Schaeffer, *GED*, p. 184. See also, Lane T. Dennis, ed., *Letters of Francis A. Schaeffer* (Westchester, Ill.: Crossway Books, 1985), pp. 70, 71 where Schaeffer identifies another weakness of the Reformation, in a letter written about 1957 as follows:

> It is my belief that the Reformation itself, with certain notable exceptions, made a basic error. . .[by making a false] division

between the intellectual and the Spiritual. (By the word Spiritual with a capital "S" we are referring to nothing less than a commitment to the Holy Spirit.). . . I think it is the "pendulum psychology" again.

The Roman Catholic Church had come to teach the *wrong* doctrines. And I feel that most of the Reformation then let the pendulum swing and thought if only the *right* doctrines were taught that all would be automatically well. Thus, to a large extent, the Reformation concentrated almost exclusively on the "teaching ministry of the Church." In other words almost all the emphasis was placed on teaching the right doctrines. In this I feel the fatal error had already been made. *It is not for a moment that we can begin to get anywhere until the right doctrines are taught. But the right doctrines mentally assented to are not an end in themselves, but should only be the vestibule to a personal and loving communion with God. . . .*

Personally I believe church history shows that as this basic weakness in Protestantism developed into a completely dead orthodoxy, then liberalism came forth. Thus, the solution is not to intellectually and coldly just shout out the right doctrines and try to shout down the false liberal doctrines. It is to go back to a cure of the basic error. It is to say "yes" to the right doctrines, and, without compromise, "no" to the wrong doctrines of both Romanism and liberalism and then to commit our lives to the practical moment by moment headship of Christ and communion of the Holy Spirit.

27. When asked in an interview when Christianity ever had had an overwhelming influence on culture, Schaeffer replied: "Never. There's no golden age. I'm tired of people who try to make me say the Reformation was a golden age. It was anything but a golden age." See Philip Yancey, "Schaeffer on Schaeffer, Part II," in *Christianity Today*, April 6, 1979, p. 25.

28. Wells, "Jeremiad," p. 18.

29. Schaeffer, *HSWTL-CW*, IV, p. 121.

30. M. A. Noll, "Rauschenbusch, Walter," *The Evangelical Dictionary of Theology*, ed. Walter A. Elwell (Grand Rapids, Mich.: Baker Book House, 1984), p. 912, 913. See further, Walter Rauschenbusch, *A Theology for the Social Gospel* (New York: Macmillan, 1917).

31. F. L. Cross, ed., *The Oxford Dictionary of the Christian Church* (1st ed.; London: Oxford University Press, 1958), p. 959. Wells goes on to mention Carl F. H. Henry and David O. Moberg, both of whom are evangelicals, as well as *Sojourners* and *The Reformed Journal*. Since he has a long quote from Niebuhr and mentions him four times (once in connection with Rauschenbusch) Niebuhr and Rauschenbusch were apparently more important sources to Wells than were Henry and Moberg.

32. Wells, "Whatever Happened," p. 13.

33. This first point of the summary would apply to Noll too. See, Noll, "Bad News," p. 27.

34. Wells concluded his essay on "Whatever Happened to Francis Schaeffer?" by admonishing Schaeffer to "eschew the siren song of media popularity" and to resist "the seduction of some whom he has helped," p. 13.

35. C. Stephen Evans, "A Misunderstood Reformer,"*Christianity Today*, September 21, 1984, p. 28. At the end of the paragraph Evans does include the following in parentheses: "(Schaeffer does admit that Kierkegaard's devotional writings can be helpful)." I did not include this part of the quote in the main body of the chapter for two reasons: First, Evans did *not* include this observation when he first presented this essay as a Wheaton College chapel address. This was added by Evans only after it was brought to his attention that he had misrepresented Schaeffer. Second, while it gives a nod to Schaeffer, it is still misleading in that it is a substantial distortion of Schaeffer's views of Kierkegaard.

36. Ron Ruegsegger, "A Reply to Gordon Clark," *Christian Scholar's Review*, XI, No. 2 (1982), p. 150.

37. Jack Rogers, "Francis Schaeffer: The Promise and the Problem (2)," *The Reformed Journal*, June 1977, p. 15.

38. Francis A. Schaeffer, *Escape From Reason* in *The Complete Works*, Vol. I (Westchester, Ill.: Crossway Books, 1982), pp. 14-16.

39. See the review of this opinion in Ron Ruegsegger, "Francis Schaeffer on Philosophy," *Christian Scholars Review*, X, No. 3 (1981), pp. 243, 244.

40. Although Ruegsegger, in *ibid*, suggests that the conclusion of some recent scholarship on Kierkegaard "is sufficient to weaken seriously Schaeffer's central argument," Gordon H. Clark points out correctly that Ruegsegger's method is unjust because he fails to show that Schaeffer is in fact wrong. See Gordon H. Clark, "A Semi-defense of Francis Schaeffer,"*Christian Scholars Review*, X, No. 2 (1982), p. 148.

41. Brand Blanshard, *Reason and Belief* (London: Allen and Unwin, 1974), Ch. 6. Alastair McKinnon makes an even stronger argument for Kierkegaard as an irrationalist in his essay "Kierkegaard, 'Paradox' and Irrationalism" in *Essays on Kierkegaard*, ed. Jerry H. Gill (Minneapolis: Burgess, 1969), pp. 102-112. In an earlier work by L. Harold DeWolf, the liberal theologian and philosopher at Boston College, *The Religious Revolt Against Reason* (New York: Harper, 1949), DeWolf is extremely critical of what he sees as Kierkegaard's "revolt against reason." DeWolf argues further that Barth, Brunner, and Reinhold Niebuhr were directly influenced by Kierkegaard's writings, and that their work is characterized by an irrationalism that extends directly back to Kierkegaard. See further Ronald H. Wells's discussion of Kierkegaard entitled "The Life of the Mind and the Way of Life" in Chapter 3 of this volume.

42. For example: ". . .religious philosopher and critic of Rationalism, is regarded as the founder of Existentialist philosophy," as quoted in *The New Encyclopedia of Britannica* (15th ed.), V, p. 803; ". . .frequently considered the first important existentialist. . ." as quoted in Alasdair MacIntyre, "Kierkegaard, Søren Aabye," *The Encyclopedia of Philosophy* (1972 ed.), III, p. 336; "Both the Dialectical Theology of K. Barth and his followers, and Existential philosophy esp. as expounded by M. Heidegger, owe their inspiration to him" in F. L. Cross, *The Oxford Dictionary of the Christian Church* (London:

Oxford University Press, 1958), p. 766. Reference works, rather than primary sources, have been cited here to demonstrate that Schaeffer's views are in fact substantiated by standard *reference works*, contrary to the claims of his critics.

43. Evans does introduce some degree of balance in this essay—e.g., he acknowledges that there may be problems in Kierkegaard's "view of the relation of faith to reason" (p. 28), and that there is no consensus concerning how Kierkegaard should be rightly understood. Evans, however, seems to tip the balance too far in the direction of uncritical approval. It would not be a good idea to "revere" Kierkegaard—or Schaeffer for that matter. The balance we need in the case of Kierkegaard is to recognize two things at once: first that there is much that is valuable in his writings; but equally, that there are serious problems concerning certain aspects of his thought, and that these problems bore bitter fruit, especially when they came to maturity in people like Heidegger and Bultmann.

44. A number of other objections to Schaeffer's work have also followed this pattern. The most important of these are stated below. In each case the false thesis raised by Schaeffer's critics is stated first and then discussed briefly:

(A) Thesis: *On the question of abortion, Schaeffer's approach is seriously defective (e.g., it is simplistic, inconsistent, etc.).* An example of this is the critique of Ron Ruegsegger which in my view borders on ethical absurdity. Ruegsegger attempts to dismiss Schaeffer's position on the grounds that he has "oversimplified a controversial issue" (because Schaeffer allegedly rests his case only on the Bible) and that he is "inconsistent" (because he actually appeals to nine "natural" arguments). (See Ron Ruegsegger, "Francis Schaeffer on Philosophy," *Christian Scholars Review*, X, No. 3 [1981], pp. 249-253.) As Gordon H. Clark points out in his critique of Ruegsegger's criticism, Schaeffer

> . . . is not inconsistent, as Ruegsegger almost sees. In opposing secular advocates of abortion and greedy politicians, it is legitimate to use *ad hominem* arguments. These arguments are legitimate even in geometry. One tries to show inconsistencies in the opponent's position. One tries to point out conclusions, logically drawn from the abortionist's principles but which he either does not like or is afraid to admit in public. In this Schaeffer commits no inconsistency.

(See Gordon H. Clark, "A Semi-defense of Francis Schaeffer," *Christian Scholars Review*, XI, No. 2 [1982], p. 149.)

In reality, there have been few people more consistent on the question of abortion than Schaeffer—whether in terms of argument, or in terms of practical involvement (see further Chapter 10 in this volume). It is particularly disturbing, however, to see someone who is trained in philosophical ethics use such a fallacious argument to discredit the views of a man who literally gave his life in trying to save the innocent unborn from being brutally killed. Moreover, it is disturbing to see someone trained in philosophical ethics with such calloused indifference. Sadly, this kind of thinking is rampant in evangelical academic circles. As Joseph Bayly observed:

> To me, the outstanding example of indifference is in our reaction to the great sin of abortion that is the shame of our nation. Each year, one-and-a-half million humans who bear the image of God are murdered, many, perhaps most of them, with accompanying great pain to which a group of non-Christian physicians recently attested. The pain is that of poisoning by a saline solution or dismemberment, being torn apart and removed in pieces from the uterus. . .
>
> Our Christian physicians [and ethicists] will be judged for their indifference. With notable exceptions the United States medical [and ethics] establishment,   including Christians, has been silent about our great national sin. . .
>
> We blame Christians in Germany during the Third Reich for their indifference to the murder of Jews. "Why were you silent?" we ask.
>
> Someday we will be asked the same question. And a righteous God will not judge the German nation without also judging our nation.
>
> God, forgive our indifference. Make us burn with white heat against injustice, especially the destruction of the weak and totally vulnerable, who bear your divine image.

(Joseph Bayly, "Our Reich of Indifference," *Eternity*, June 1984, p. 56.)

(B) Thesis: *Schaeffer has become the captive of the ideological right.* This thesis fails to take into account Schaeffer's strong and consistent stand over the years against *all* kinds of authoritarianism (whether from the right or the left); it also fails to recognize Schaeffer's distinction between being "cobelligerents" and "allies." (See, *The Church at the End of the Twentieth Century*, in *The Complete Works*, Vol. 4 [Westchester, Ill.: Crossway Books, 1982], pp. 30-31.) Schaeffer also thought it was fine for some areas of economic life to be nationalized (like the railroads in Switzerland). Schaeffer's views in this area are too complex and sophisticated for his opponents to discredit them by defining him as "right wing," or "new right," etc. In reality, it seems that this kind of criticism is little more than an ideological response from the evangelical left. The rhetoric of the evangelical left is especially evident, for example, in Richard V. Pierard, "The Unmaking of Francis Schaeffer: An Evangelical Tragedy," *The Wittenburg Door*, April-May 1984, pp. 29, 31; and Ronald A. Wells, "Jeremiad," pp. 15, 16. See further, Darryl G. Hart, "The Schaeffer Gap," *The Reformed Journal*, October 1983, pp. 6, 7; and Mark A Noll, "When Bad," p. 27. For an insightful critique of the ideology of the evangelical left see Clark H. Pinnock, "A Pilgrimage in Political Theology," in Ronald Nash, *Liberation Theology* (Milford, Mich.: Mott Media, 1984), pp. 45-67. One of the main points of Pinnock's critique is the basic alienation of the evangelical left, which finds expression especially in its hostility toward democratic capitalism and its romantic affirmation of the ideals of the left.

(C) Thesis: *Schaeffer was wrong in saying that inerrancy is the only consistent evangelical view, and in saying that many evangelicals hold to a "weakened view" of Scripture.* This thesis has been advanced, for example, by Jack Rogers in "Francis Schaeffer: The Promise and the Problem (2)," p. 17. Rogers's thesis, however, has been totally discredited by John D. Woodbridge in *Biblical Authority: A Critique of the Rogers/McKim Proposal* (Grand Rapids, Mich.: Zondervan, 1982); the full statement of Rogers's view on "limited inerrancy" was presented in Jack Rogers and Donald McKim, *The Authority and Interpretation of the Bible: An Historical Approach* (New York: Harper and Row, 1979). Related to this is the view of George Marsden that Biblical inerrancy as generally held by conservative Christians today is a novel belief which emerged in the eighteenth and nineteenth centuries, and should not be seen therefore as a normative criterion of what it means to be an evangelical. Marsden expresses this theme in various chapters of *Fundamentalism and American Culture: The Shaping of Twentieth-Century Evangelicalism: 1870-1925* (New York: Oxford University Press, 1980), pp. 55-62, 111-116. As Woodbridge and others have demonstrated, however, this view cannot be sustained. (See for example John D. Woodbridge's unpublished essay entitled "Francis Schaeffer's Perception of Contemporary Evangelicalism: An Assessment.") In contrast to Marsden, the perceptive sociological study of James Davison Hunter sees inerrancy as an essential characteristic of evangelicalism (see *American Evangelicalism: Conservative Religion and the Quandary of Modernity* [New Brunswick, N.J.: Rutgers University Press, 1983], esp. pp. 139-141). Hunter sees the greatest threat to evangelicalism coming from evangelical accommodation to modernity, observing that "on the issue of inerrancy, the rumblings have already begun to sound," p. 132.

(D) Thesis: *There really are two Schaeffers: the "early Schaeffer" who made a very positive contribution; and the "later Schaeffer," who went wrong somewhere along the way.* Since it would take a comprehensive analysis of Schaeffer's work to substantiate or refute this thesis, only a few things can be mentioned here. First, Schaeffer did not accept this view himself. He believed there was continuity in his work from beginning to end. At the same time he did acknowledge some change in emphasis and strategy, due to the changing context in Western culture. As a result of my own comprehensive study of Schaeffer's letters and his other works, I would conclude that there is only "one Schaeffer" from the mid-1950s until his death in 1984. We do find, of course, considerable development and some change in focus, but the emphasis is on continuity rather than discontinuity. For those who have wanted to distinguish between the (good) "early Schaeffer" and the (bad) "later Schaeffer," the distinction cannot be sustained. The "two Schaeffers" are the same person, whose early views were essentially the same as his later ones. It would seem that those who hold to the "two Schaeffers" thesis do so not because of a significant change in Schaeffer, but because of a shift in their own views—that is, since their own views have moved away from Schaeffer's views, they are no longer comfortable with his views and have propounded the

Schaeffer: An Evangelical Tragedy") and Ronald A. Wells ("Whatever Happened to Francis Schaeffer?").

(E) Thesis: *Schaeffer's basic approach is essentially a new form of rationalism.* Although some have made this assertion, it represents a fundamental misunderstanding of Schaeffer's views. Most of his books provide ample evidence to the contrary. This issue, however, is dealt with specifically in Francis A. Schaeffer, *The God Who Is There* in *The Complete Works*, Vol. I (Westchester, Ill.: Crossway Books, 1982), pp. 175-187, esp. pp. 183-185.

Although thesis A-E in the notes above could be handled only briefly, we see evidence of the same pattern noted in the main text whereby Schaeffer's critics have attempted to raise objections to his work. The steps in this outline are again: (1) a basic criticism is made of Schaeffer's work in a particular area; (2) Schaeffer's view in this area is then presented in a way which is substantially false; (3) the false understanding of Schaeffer's view is then shown by Schaeffer's critic to be "untenable"; (4) the critic then presents his own "tenable" view; (5) upon inspection, however, it is the critics "tenable" view (not Schaeffer's "untenable" view) which turns out to be seriously defective. This is not to say that Schaeffer's views are beyond dispute. There will be errors of detail and differences of interpretation in everyone's work. But the point is that the objections discussed here, which represent those most commonly made of Schaeffer, have not been sustained, and that his views deserve to be handled in a more responsible manner.

45. Schaeffer, *The God Who Is There* in *The Complete Works*, Vol. I, pp. 185-187.

46. Stephen Board, "The Rise of Francis Schaeffer," *Eternity*, June 1977, p. 40.

47. Schaeffer, *The God Who Is There* in *The Complete Works*, Vol. I, p. 187.

48. *Ibid.*, p. 186.

49. A personal letter written in August of 1983.

50. Some of the strongest appreciation for Schaeffer's work has come from outside evangelical circles. For example, the late Roman Catholic Bishop, Fulton Sheen once observed: "[Francis Schaeffer's] summary of philosophical doctrines is one of the best I have ever read, and I taught philosophy in graduate school for twenty-five years" ("Bottom-Line Theology: An Interview With Fulton J. Sheen," *Christianity Today*, June 3, 1977, p. 9). Similarly, Keith Mano in *National Review* remarked that "Schaeffer is a powerful and accurate summarizer" (as quoted in Board, "The Rise of Francis Schaeffer," p. 40).

51. C. S. Lewis, "Christianity and Culture," in *Christian Reflections* (Grand Rapids, Mich.: William B. Eerdmans, 1967), p. 33.

52. Schaeffer, *The God Who Is There* in *The Complete Works*, Vol. I, p. 140.

53. *Ibid.*, p. 140, 141.

54. *Ibid.*, p. 141, 142.

55. Lewis, "Christianity and Culture," p. 29.

56. Other dangers of being a specialist could be developed further. Some of these include: (1) the danger of looking to the secular world for acceptance, recognition, and approval of one's work; (2) the danger of allowing one's discipline to become "autonomous," so that one's specialty stands in judgment of Scripture rather than the other way around; (3) the danger of "academic detachment," "indifference," and the failure to be active in the critical issues of the day (see e.g., Chapter 6, Note 44-D).

Chapter 8 / The Quiet Assurance of Truth

1. I am grateful to Mary Lou Sather, a close friend of the Schaeffers, for many of the details in this story.

2. This point was mentioned to me especially by Dr. Charles Kennedy, a close friend of the family and the chairman of the first Rochester L'Abri Conference in 1980. I also appreciate the ideas used as background for this essay from Dr. Schaeffer's personal physician and friend, Dr. Robert M. Petitt of Mayo Clinic; and his personal nurse the last weeks of his life, Mrs. Diane Drugg.

3. See my book *Francis Schaeffer: The Man and His Message* (Wheaton, Ill.: Tyndale House, 1985), Chapters 7-20, for a full development of this point.

4. *Ibid.*, chapters 1-6.

5. A. W. Tozer, *God Tells the Man Who Cares* (Harrisburg, Penn.: Christian Publications, 1970), pp. 100-102.

Chapter 10 / We Thought We Could Have It All

1. Francis A. Schaeffer, *He Is There and He Is Not Silent* in *The Complete Works of Francis A. Schaeffer*, Vol. I. (Westchester, Ill.: Crossway Books, 1982), p. 285.

2. Francis A. Schaeffer, *Back to Freedom and Dignity* in *The Complete Works of Francis A. Schaeffer*, Vol. I (Westchester, Ill.: Crossway Books, 1982), p. 367.

3. Francis A. Schaeffer, *Whatever Happened to the Human Race?* (Westchester, Ill.: Crossway Books, 1983), p. 87.

Chapter 11 / By Teaching, By Life, and By Action

1. Francis Schaeffer, *How Should We Then Live?* in *The Complete Works of Francis Schaeffer*, Vol. V (Westchester, Ill.: Crossway Books, 1982), p. 218, 219.

2. *Ibid.*, p. 222.

3. *Ibid.*, p. 219, 220.

4. *Ibid.*, p. 243.

5. *Ibid.*, p. 254.

6. Francis Schaeffer, *A Christian Manifesto* in *The Complete Works of Francis Schaeffer*, Vol. V (Westchester, Ill.: Crossway Books, 1982), p. 468, 469.

7. *Ibid.*, p. 496.

Chapter 12 / Truth and Oppression

1. Prabhu Guptara, *Indian Spirituality* (Bramcote, Notts., England: Grove Books, 1984), p. 22.

2. *A Decade of TRACI* [pamphlet] (New Delhi: Theological Research and Communication Institute, n.d.). Further information concerning the Theological Research and Communication Institute may be obtained by writing to: TRACI, E-537, Greater Kailash II, New Delhi-110 048, India.

3. Further information concerning the Indian Ground Works Trust may be obtained by writing to: Mr. Prabhu Guptara, Indian Ground Works Trust, Pine View, 58 Ridgeway Road, Farnham, Surrey, England GU9 8NS.

4. From Vishal and Ruth Mangalwadi's printed letter to friends and supporters, May 24, 1985.

5. For more information about TRACI, ACRA, KSS and related projects, Vishal Mangalwadi may be contacted at the following address: E-537 Greater Kailash II, New Delhi-110 048, India.

6. See further, Francis A. Schaeffer, *The Great Evangelical Disaster* (Westchester, Ill.: Crossway Books, 1984), pp. 111-115.

7. Guptara, *op. cit.*, pp. 22, 23.

8. See the chapter titled "No Little People, No Little Places," from Francis A. Schaeffer's book *No Little People* in *The Complete Works of Francis A. Schaeffer*, Vol. III (Westchester, Ill.: Crossway Books, 1982), pp. 5-191. Vishal Mangalwadi first heard "No Little People, No Little Places" when it was presented by Dr. Schaeffer as a sermon when Mangalwadi was at L'Abri.

9. *Ibid.*, p. 8.

10. *Ibid.*, p. 8, 9.

11. *Ibid.*, p. 186.

12. *Ibid.*, p. 184.

13. *Ibid.*, p. 186.

Books by Francis A. Schaeffer

1. In the early 1950s Dr. Schaeffer did publish a booklet explaining his understanding of the Bible's teaching on baptism. This has been out of print now for many years. Schaeffer did not want this to be brought back in print nor included in the *Complete Works* because he did not want the method of baptism to become a divisive issue among Christians and thereby distract them from what were to Schaeffer more essential concerns of Christian faith.

Books by Edith Schaeffer

1. In addition to the two biographical works by Edith Schaeffer, a full-scale biography is scheduled for publication in 1987 by Crossway Books. Also available is a popular treatment of Schaeffer by L. G. Parkhurst entitled *Francis Schaeffer: The Man and His Message* (Wheaton, Ill.: Tyndale House, 1985).